New Memories of the MILLENNIUM Two

by Bob Bartos

Library of Congress Control Number: 2002090542

ISBN: 1-57579-238-9

Printed in the United States of America
PINE HILL PRESS
4000 West 57th Street
Sioux Falls, S.D. 57106

Dedicated

To: My wife Frances of 57 years, my two daughters Nancy and Terri and my only son Rocky and second son Larry Hoover all of whom I'm very proud.

To: All the *Reporter and Farmer* subscribers who read my stories, and even those who don't.

To: The *Reporter and Farmer* publishers. Editors John Suhr and LeAnn Suhr without whom there would be no book or column, and also the professional staff that I cause more problems for, than help.

To: Webster, S.D. my life-time home town and all the people who live there or have lived here.

Thank You!

Bob Bartos

Acknowledgements

I would like to inform the readers of this column that I'm a scribbler, not a writer. I don't use the proper words or sentence structure. My spelling is detective work, for the best educated person to decipher and without the expertise of LeAnn Suhr, my stories would not be readable. I don't write fiction, all my stories have a factual background.

Also my wife Frances, who puts up with a turned off TV while I scribble stories and cleans up all the waste paper and half-filled pages I crumple up on the floor in our home.

Jeanette Knock and the entire staff of Pine Hill Press whose professional help in assembling this book at a price I and my readers could afford—it isn't easy working with a novice writer.

Table of Contents

Preface

First and foremost—every story you read in this book has a factual background. I don't write fiction. At my age of nearly 80 years, a lot of my sources are deceased, but I try to mention enough names so the locals can check them out.

Since my first book *Memories of the Millennium,* with only twenty stories, my column readers have requested another book. *New Memories of the Millennium Two* has over fifty new columns, two and a half more new short stories. If you enjoyed the first book you'll get two and a half times more smiles out of *New Memories of the Millennium Two*, but not at two and a half times the price, it's $16.00. That includes shipping, postage and handling. They make the perfect gift and I'll gladly sign them. All of the stories are original humorous happenings and history of local origin from Webster, Day County, South Dakota.

Memories of the Millennium sold out—no reprints. Keep a copy, they are very treasured. *Memories of the Millennium Two* is also a limited printing. I hope to sell them out quickly, recoup my printing cost and get started on *New Memories of the Millennium Three*. Read the stories carefully. Your name may be in it. I'm sure if you lived in Webster you'll know or have heard about the people in the stories. Hoping you'll enjoy and recall old memories as much as I have writing about them.

Thank You!

Bob Bartos

To order additional copies
of this book call or write:

Bob Bartos
Box 93
Webster, S.D. 57274
(605) 345-3779

They make the perfect gift,
and I'll sign and personalize each copy!

The roots of Lawrence Welk's orchestra

Let me warn my column readers, this will be a series of columns about a wealthy, famous music man, Lawrence Welk, whose musical career in Webster, Waubay and Roslyn laid the very foundation for his rise to fame. The first five years of his musical career were developed with Webster area musicians. From the very beginning to this day, there has always been at least one featured band member playing a huge role in his success—and history should record it that way.

Here's my story. It all began last week when three gals in three different locations, three different times said something like this—"It's always been a dream of mine to dance with Lawrence Welk." Even the librarian made a similar comment when I checked out Lawrence Welk's autobiography, only to find there's no mention about his first real money-making band in the Day County area or any of great talented Webster area musicians who played with him at the very start. People like Homer Schmidt, drummer, played with him for over six years. Leo Fortin, Waubay is mentioned but not in the beginning years—even though Leo was with him from the beginning for 22 years, was featured musician in his band. People like saxophone player Lampert Wattier, accordionist Alvin Johnson, piano player Ernie Skadvold, accordionists Florian Ewalt and Herman Waller, and Aubrey French on the coronet. These men and many more from the Webster area made up his band for almost five years in the early days of his career.

Lawrence Welk, born in Strasburg, ND March 11, 1903, by his own admission was a dummer esel (dumb donkey)—not much good at farm work or school—he quit in fourth grade. Going to town at 13, he saw a man with a big fancy piano accordion, playing on stage—and the hat full of money he got for playing. All he could think of was getting a fancy accordion, being on stage, people paying and applauding him—a fantasy that would stay with him all his life. He had already proved to his family he would never be a farmer. At 16 his father bought him a fancy $400 accordion for his promise to work on the farm for four years and that he would learn to play it and make money playing for weddings and church doings to help pay for it. He took some lessons from a man in Strasburg, who right out told him he lacked the talent to be a good accordion player. But he was smart enough to get other kids to play for him in little dance band groups of three or four.

On his 21st birthday, March 11, 1924, he left home with a ticket for Aberdeen to stay with relatives who had two boys who played drums and violin. They played for church doings, weddings and a barn dance—putting together a five-piece band and somehow making a deal with the manager of Tacoma Park pavilion on a ticket percentage deal to play for a dance. That Sunday afternoon, seeing all the people in the area, he thought this would be his big break—not knowing there was a big area baseball game to be played at the same time. No crowd showed up. But when it started to rain the crowd rushed for shelter and Welk made enough money to pay the band and buy a used Chevy. He headed east and with car trouble and no money left, arrived in Webster.

Now here's how Charlie Bailly and Atlas Knapp recall Lawrence Welk in 1925, just over a year off the farm. A well mannered man, polite, shy, who smiled a lot. Sort of clumsy, couldn't talk—only broken English. Always broke. In fact, Frank Lewno, who repaired his car never got paid before Welk left town. Frank talked about that until he died. Ask Roman Czmowski or Ron Kennedy. Later, Frank said the unpaid bill was worth it to him—just knowing a millionaire owed him money.

Welk's first job in Webster was playing for his supper at Knapp's Cafe. Strapping on his big fancy accordion he became the great entertainer—a changed man. Playing fancy flourishes up and down the keyboard, a few chords with no timing and rhythm, a few waltz notes mixed in. People like Florian Ewalt and Herman Waller, great accordion and concertina players, said they were more impressed with the accordion he was trying to play than the music coming out of it.

Next he talked Charlie Bailly, owner of the Lyric Theater, into letting him play for half an hour before the silent movie started. Charlie said he was like a first class con man, telling Charlie to charge five cents more a ticket, splitting it with him, a built-in promoter. Proof! An exaggerated ad in the Oct. 20, 1925 Reporter & Farmer. Mr. Lawrence Wilk (they misspelled his name) who has played for many dances in the area will play his piano accordion at the Lyric Theater Sunday night. (I don't consider Aberdeen in our area or a couple of dances many.)

In the meantime, Welk had contacted men like Webster's Homer Schmidt, Alvin Johnson, Florian Ewalt, Herman Waller, Lampert Wattier; Waubay's Leo Fortin, Ernie Skadvold and Aubrey French—almost everyone who had played for area barn dances—forming a five piece dance band. He would get dance dates, make and peddle dance bills, pay them and furnish the car. He would be band leader and it would be called Lawrence Welk's Orchestra with his picture always on the dance bill. He was a great promoter, keeping all the guys who wanted to play, making more money playing for him than on their own.

But soon, Leo Fortin and Homer Schmidt would find out Lawrence Welk was a big faker as a musician. He could hardly speak English, couldn't read or write, sing or play his accordion hardly at all. He would stand in front of the band directing the others. It would be Leo who would tell Welk, "All you have to do is strap that accordion on, go one, two, three to start us off and let us play. Every time you start playing you throw us off our rhythm and timing." And so Welk started his trademark—stomping his foot, counting and directing the 5 piece band like a 27-piece orchestra. Just like he always dreamed it would be. Smiling at the dancers, watching what tunes brought the most applause. One thing was for sure, nobody ever attended a Lawrence Welk dance without having a good time.

Next week, Welk changes the name of the band. Some of the local guys quit. Welk expands his area to South Dakota's big towns, but only with local Webster area help, laying the foundation for his fantasy of being a great band leader, which was a long way from reality in the mid-1920s.

A great band leader dances with the ladies

It was the Webster and Waubay men in Lawrence Welk's early band days who would lay the foundation and trademarks he used to reach his dream of being a great band leader—rich and famous.

It was at Darby Davis' barn dance, Welk directing the band, Leo Fortin the joking trumpet player said, "Lawrence, why don't you go dance with some of the girls sitting on the sidelines while we play this next set." After a lot of prodding he jumped off stage and just like everything else, he was an awkward dancer. The first girl pulled away from him after only a few steps. But soon another girl—who could follow anybody—felt sorry for him and helped him out. Leo stated later that soon girls started coming up to the stage asking him to dance. The crowd loved it—and the thrill the girls got! Even in the early days. Telling everyone the next day, "I danced with the band leader!" That also was going to be a Welk trademark for the next 50 years. I don't care what anyone says, Lawrence Welk was a clumsy dancer right up to his last days on national television. But the flowing skirts of the professional dancers that he surrounded himself with made him look reasonable dancing a few steps—not great, like he imagined himself.

I have to admire Lawrence Welk's fantasy dream. With no musical or other abilities, only a $400 accordion which he couldn't play well, yet in his own mind, he thought himself the great band leader. Like Charlie Bailly, the theater owner told him after playing a half hour before the movie started. "Welk, get a lot of band backup to drown you out when you play, because by yourself you're lousy." It must have sunk in, because Lawrence Welk always wore his accordion but there was always another accordion player who really knew how to play backing him up in any band he put together from early days to the present time. Roslyn's Myron Floren holds that job today.

Lawrence Welk was a great promoter and salesman, greater than his claim to fame as a musician. He had an ear for tunes people liked to hear and dance to. He knew when people were having a good time. He lived for applause and the amount of applause the band got for the tune being played. He kept standing by old favorites— polkas, waltzes, schottisches.

But the depression was coming. Welk had expanded his territory and the local men were tiring of four or five hours traveling to dance dates, returning home to their regular jobs. They had no dreams of going big time—except drummer Homer Schmidt and Leo Fortin, the featured two-trumpet playing man from Waubay. Both were very talented, could read music and were professional caliber. Leo Fortin would remain with Welk off and on until 1950, when another area man, Myron Floren from Roslyn would take over guiding Welk to fame and fortune. But for now, Lawrence Welk, always the promoter, changed the name of the band from Lawrence Welk Orchestra with his picture on the dance bill to Lawrence Welk's Novelty Band with Leo Fortin's picture—a little smaller than his—on the dance bill. Later it would be the Hotsy-Totsy Boys, but the music the band played didn't change much. As the depression and dirty-thirties got worse, smaller dance crowds at the Mitchell Corn Palace, Watertown's Casino Ballroom, Aberdeen's Roof Garden. So Welk was going to take his six-piece band out of state—to Texas. Bigger towns, bigger crowds. He lined up a few dates for the band, but Fortin and the other band members, Schmidt too, decided Welk was always going to be a barn dance man. He was holding them back from big time. The oompah music was changing to swing and they were going to Chicago. The band quit after that night's performance. Welk was left stranded. With dance dates to fill. He got another band together, filled the dates and headed back to South Dakota. He put together another band at Yankton, playing on WNAX radio for $60 a week. Now called Lawrence Welk's America's Greatest Little Band.

Between feed and seed and hog tonic commercials he would advertise his dance dates. Playing in a soundproof studio was a lot different than playing in a noisy dance hall where you can miss a note or two and no one notices it. Also, in a radio studio Welk wasn't seen or needed waving his arms leading the band. He couldn't speak English, couldn't stamp his foot to start the band because the control room guy would throw him out and couldn't play because the band had to sound good over the radio. Welk was reduced to excess baggage—a very unhappy man dreaming of guys in Webster. Like Aubrey French, the horn player at whose home he lived while in Webster—the house located at 717 West Second Street. He called on Florian Ewalt to fill in on accordion on his radio show. It really all began with Webster musicians—now it was falling apart.

Soon, here comes Leo Fortin, the mainstay of Welk's former band, fresh from Chicago big-time to save Welk again.

Telling Welk how the big bands operated 16-20 piece bands, swing sounds and he knew of a lot of piano arrangers and music writers. The big dinner clubs, cover charges and most of the big bands had sponsors—companies that paid to have the band advertise their products. Fortin knew Welk's faults and assets too, of being a great promoter. Fortin was one man the strong-headed Welk would listen to. Leo Fortin, the Waubay man, sort of took over the band playing. Welk the great promoter needed a sponsor. He was broke. He needed a new touring car to haul the band. Finding a fledgling chewing gum company in California by telephone, Welk the super salesman, with much exaggeration—told them about Lawrence Welk's greatest Little Band playing the midwest, WNAX radio show, how he could open their product sales up in the whole midwest, where his orchestra played.

Next week Welk gets a sponsor—and some more big problems which again, Webster area men help him solve, getting him on the road to big time. It's my opinion Lawrence Welk's musical fame foundation was made not in Strasburg, ND or any place other than right here in Webster, Day County, South Dakota. And it should be part of our history—or at least recorded as great memories of the millennium. This will become more apparent to readers next week.

With local help, Welk fulfills his dream

Lawrence Welk in the early 1930s, depression years, needed a sponsor to pay the bills. As Leo Fortin, returning from Chicago big time to rejoin the band and WNAX, Yankton had suggested. Welk taking Leo's advice, gave an exaggerated telephone pitch to the fledgling Honolulu Fruit Gum Company. They sent an advertising man to check him out in Yankton. Welk was an outstanding business promoter and before the meeting ended had a new big touring car with advertising written on both sides. Lawrence Welk's Honolulu Fruit orchestra. To close the deal he became the midwest distributor for Honolulu Fruit Gum. He even sold to stores in small towns his band played in. He also sold gum at five cents a pack from the bandstand which would cause Welk's band problems. It would cost ballrooms about as much money to clean up the chewing gum mess after Welk's Honolulu Fruit Gum Orchestra played than the profit they made hiring the band in the first place. Also, the band, which was getting more talented and bigger, was getting fed up playing for a fruit gum outfit. Wearing crepe paper leis, white shirts and straw hats. Sweating all night, fading colors staining their white shirts. As Leo Fortin said, Made us look like a Honolulu sunrise.

Welk, with 19-20 salesmen working for him was making more money with gum than his band. But he decided to give it up and sold out to carry on his dream of being a big time band leader.

Welk was the first person to put painted advertising on a new car. Now, buying a sleeper bus, one of the first bands to do so, with bunks along the wall. It looked more like a cattle truck. With outstanding musical talent like Leo Fortin playing two trumpets at once, the feature attraction from Waubay and a great piano talent in Loren Loe from the Pierpont area, who would later go on to play with Charlie Barnett's big tie swing band in the east he had put together one of the best bands in the midwest. It was time to go big time.

Welk promoted his first big booking in the St. Paul Hotel following big bands like Les Brown. Then on to other big towns. Now Lawrence Welk was leading the big band. Everyone doing everything for him. He was becoming the maestro of his fantasy dream.

The last change of Welk's band's many names would come from a fan letter stating the band sounded so light, bubbly and sparkling. One of Welk's PR men came up with (in the 40s) music like champagne. Soon the name, Lawrence Welk's Champagne Music. This while he had just completed a stand at the Penn Hotel, following the Glenn Miller Band, whose hit song was Pennsylvania 6-5000, the hotel's phone number. There was a plaque on the wall in the Penn Hotel in 1974 saying the name champagne music for Welk's band originated there.

Playing big hotels and ballrooms in the United States, Welk would always come back to South Dakota to play a tour, making a stop at Waubay's Legion Hall. Leo Fortin's home town, with Jayne Walton as his champagne lady. A big time band playing in Waubay! Why not?

In the late '40s and early '50s TV was the big money place to go Welk had not hit the real big time. He needed a TV sponsorship and again, it would be a Day County man to come to his aid. Leo Fortin. Leo was a fun guy to be around off stage and on stage too. Welk, because of Leo's talent, gave Leo a lot of leeway. He was the life of the party during band breaks. All the big shot executives would gather around him. One of these big wheels became a drinking friend of Leo's. He was on the advertising staff of Miller Beer Company, whose trademark was The Champagne of Bottled Beer. When someone said, Look at that the champagne of bottled beer guy drinking with a champagne music maker. Soon the talk was Miller Hi-Life beer spending millions on television advertising nationwide. Of course Leo Fortin took the idea to Welk, who made a deal to go to Los Angeles to complete a TV program for Miller Beer. After that would be Dodge Motors. The rest is history.

Leo Fortin would quit Welk for the last time, not wanting to go to the coast. It would be at this time another Day County man would take over and guide the Lawrence Welk Band. Myron Floren of Roslyn. After 22 years of playing for Welk, Leo Fortin would return to teach music and form a great little band in the Watertown area, using some of the old time members of Welk's Day County Band. Those who started the foundation for Welk's fantasy dream in the '30s.

Again, from Lawrence Welk's very beginning, a Day County man or men have laid the very foundation for his big band goals and lifetime fantasy of being a band leader. He calls Myron Floren his right-hand man and he is. But he never acknowledges help from other Webster area men who gave him the real early start.

A dummer esel with a fantasy dream (his own words) Lawrence Welk was in the beginning and up to the end music and business' greatest promoter of all times. Largest playing big band leader Lawrence Welk, champagne music maker and Day County music men from the beginning to end helped him get there.

Information for these stories came from Lawrence Welk's autobiography, Atlas Knapp, Charles Bailey Sr., Florian Ewalt's sons Joe and John, Alvin Johnson, Charles Gurney, owner of WNAX radio he was my commanding officer in 1943, Roman Czmowski and people I may have forgotten to mention. Like Donnie Fortin, a classmate in Waubay in the 1930s.

My story of Lawrence Welk inserts unrecorded or left out parts of the written history I've researched that are not acknowledged by any Lawrence Welk material and to somewhat expose the claim of Day County and the Webster area in Lawrence Welk's rise to fame.

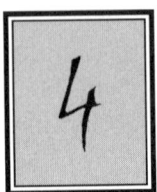

Myron Floren—
best accordion man ever

Day County has produced a lot of famous people—one of the longest lasting for 70 years is Myron Floren, also known nationwide as the accordion man with Lawrence Welk's orchestra, for the last 50 years on national tv.

Myron was born Nov. 5, 1919 in Roslyn. The Floren family became well known when their father ran for county treasurer in 1936, but even before that, at eight years old, Myron and his sister Valborg were talented enough to play for wedding and social functions in the Roslyn area. Myron was on a button box and Valborg on piano. At 12 years old Myron was considered better than most of the old-timers playing in the area. He was already studying by note rather than by ear, playing piano, organ and accordion.

Myron Floren's second accordion after his Wards $19.95 button box was a piano one. He kept borrowing it from Jake Holland, a Roslyn farm neighbor in the late 30s. One day, while returning the accordion, Jake suggested Myron was playing the accordion more than he was and could play it better than he could, maybe he should own it. It wasn't long after that Jake had a cow and Myron owned a piano accordion rather than a button box (which is stored in Myron's garage today in California).

By the time Myron had reached high school he was already a solo performer. He played at the Day County Fair in 1931 at 12 years old and played in make up dance bands for area entertainment making $2 a night—all the while doing farm chores and going to school. He was a very busy boy, when his dad decided to leave the farm and run for Day County treasurer in 1936. Myron and his sister on piano played for every Democratic township meeting in Day County and sometimes a dance afterward. Upon meeting Sigurd Anderson, he wondered how such a nice guy could be a Republican! Everybody in the county knew the Florens. Sometimes a cousin, Earl Nerland played drums.

Before I write any more, Roslyn is the hometown of Myron Floren. His childhood memories are there and 10 1/2 years of his schooling. Now I'm going to write about him and his family as I know it—in Webster from 1936-38.

I was a freshman in high school when Myron Floren was a Webster High School senior. His brother Arlie was the guy I looked up to—a wild sort of guy who could take anything driveable apart. Putting it back together was something else. It would always start but wouldn't run long. My best memory of Arlie is about a two-popper Indian motorcycle he acquired. It had to be pushed more than rode because the chain drive kept breaking. It was by Joe Arbach's tavern and gas station—on old Highway 12, the Yellowstone Trail, located where the laundromat is now. The road was all gravel and wet from recent rain. I was riding in back of Arlie as we went downhill. Hitting loose gravel, we went into the ditch, through a barbed wire fence and ended up in sister Aloysius' pie plant patch (called rhubarb today). Other than a few gravel burns and a couple of small cuts we were alright but the smell of rhubarb lingered for weeks afterwards in the cycle as Arlie tried to repair it. That rhubarb patch was located close to the two plum bushes in the right rough in the center of number one fairway of the Webster golf course. Every time my ball lands there, which is often, I think of that motorcycle ride and Arlie Floren.

Meanwhile, Myron was studying, making accordion arrangements, developing new polkas and writing songs for piano accordion, because no classical or band arrangements for his instrument were included in high school or college bands. In order for Myron Floren to get into the Webster district music contest he would sing a solo, "Come to the Fair," and win first place. That sort of ended his singing. He played the organ, piano and in college viola—to play with the college orchestra. Even though he would go on to college, while being a big hit on KSOO-KELO Sioux Falls as "The Melody Man" he was a professional. Also, he had started Floren Accordion School with well over 75 students. He married one of them. He was very busy and making money even as a college freshman in 1939. He was also working clearing dishes at Augustana College to help his tuition.

Let's get back to Webster. Myron would play every chance he could get in public, paid or not. One band that accepted him with open arms was the Webster Booster Band. Myron would make his accordion sounds fit in anywhere and make the whole band sound great. I'll name a few Booster Band members he played with—J.W. Headley, James Rathbun Sr. and Jr., Dr. Warren Sewell and brother Steve, Jay Wickre, Jolly Johnson, Dr. Farris Pfister, Leonard Langager, Floyd Cornwell, Ned Harris and others. In 1937-38 Myron was a regular in the band.

Myron was very sought after to sit in with area dance bands—like the Henning group from Grenville and Dakota Ramblers—Herman Czmowski, Lambert Wattier, Paul Gebur, Alvin Johnson and Florian Ewalt.

And besides all that he spent a lot of time recovering from a bout with rheumatic fever.

He still had time as a 16-17 year old guy to think about girls. I know he had a crush on a Roslyn girl, Carol Strand, but in Webster I don't know of any girls he dated. His standards may have been a little high as his sisters were very good looking. One, Virginia, would go on after leaving Webster in 1941 to live in Sioux Falls and become Washington High School's 1945 homecoming queen.

Virginia wrote a book about her life in Roslyn and her best friend Myron, called Dear Friend. It's got a chapter on bedbugs that's a zinger, and a whole chapter on Webster and her school friends—mostly in grade school—Joyce Sigdestad, Jean Wang, Opal Kjos (Mrs. Leo Gebur), Gene Carlis, Clarence Dedrickson, Kay Bloom, Ramona Fiksdal, Barb Sakariason (Mrs. Ray Ninke), Raydon and Richard Christianson, Clarence Sauer and many others.

Everybody has stories to tell about the Florens—mostly about Myron, the famous one. Some founded, some unfounded. One thing for sure, everyone in Roslyn and some in Webster can claim to be a relative, no matter how distant a cousin or marriage it might be. Everyone wants to claim him, of course, no matter how famous or how long. Myron Floren carries on. He's now close to 82 years old. No greater respect can any man receive from Roslyn, Webster or Day County. He became the best in the world at what he does—playing a piano accordion—and made it a very respected instrument of music. Some of his dozen copyrighted songs and polkas, played and arranged by Myron Floren with Lawrence Welk's band were written while he was a senior at Webster High School. One for sure was Dakota Polka, and he still gets royalties off that one. And many more.

Myron Floren always remembers his first new Scprani piano accordion in 1937, from Wes Cook's music store in Webster, SD.

Skinny Aberdeen
kid makes good

This skinny kid with a white shirt, collar open, sleeves half rolled up was going door-to-door in our block with pamphlet in hand. It was a hot August afternoon and he was coming up my sidewalk—not even taking a shortcut across the neighbor's lawn. As I opened the door he said, "I'm Tom Daschle, running for congress," looking me straight in the eye. Well, kid, come on in. I don't need all this outside hot air in the house. He sort of smiled and chuckled. Congress and hot air, he must have thought. He looked tired. His white shirt was a little damp with sweat.

Where you from? "Aberdeen." You got a chance to get elected? "Sure have," he said, "if I can count on your vote." Now let's get one thing straight. I don't believe in politicians or politics. Again, looking me straight in the eye, this skinny kid said, "Sir, you should!" Before I could straighten this kid out my wife and son came into the room, my wife saying, "Come, have something cool to drink."

"I'm Tom Daschle, ma'am. I'm asking for your vote. I'm running for congress." As he stuck out his hand to my son, a freshman home from college, they engaged in some college chatter. "You registered to vote?" he asked my son. When he got a negative reply, he pulled out a registration card and asked if he would like to be a registered voter. My son said sure. Not knowing I was a registered Democrat, my wife Republican (we like to stay neutral) it came time to place an X in the box on the registration card Tom Daschle was filling out for my son. "You're registering Democrat?" "No," my son replied, "Republican." Shocked and surprised, I was embarrassed! Tom here is running as a Democrat for congress, I said. Now, feeling sorry for Tom Daschle. Everyone was soon put very much at ease, as Tom moved his pen from the Democratic to

Republican box for his X. "You can vote for me after I win the primary," he said with a smile.

My son was not registering Democrat because most of his friends were Republicans at that time, he said. Not because he had strong political beliefs.

Tom Daschle, the skinny kid had impressed me, my wife and son with his soft spoken manner and the way he took charge and handled a most embarrassing situation. Shaking hands as he left, he said thanks for the visit. And reminding my son, "I'm counting on your Republican vote after I win the primary. I sure would appreciate it. And your Republican registration card will be turned in to the Day County Courthouse before I leave this afternoon."

Through news reports I've kept track of Tom Daschle, the skinny kid from Aberdeen. And I bet that's the only time he ever put an X in a Republican box. But I liked that kid from the first time I met him. I'm not a political person and could care less, but as a person, Tom does his job and stands by his beliefs—whether you agree or not. He gets the job done in a soft spoken manner. My son's registration as a republican was turned in, along with I assume a lot of Democrat ones. He won the primary and my son voted for him, as my wife and I did. Just because we liked this kid, not knowing where his political career would take him.

Just to show you how political I am, I like George W. Bush because when the secret service guys surrounding his dad pushed me aside at the Houston Open golf tourney, it was this kid (now president) who came over with his quirky smile and said, "Sorry about that fellow. Things get a little crowded around Dad (who was then president)."

And I like Billy Janklow. He came up the hard way, made something of himself, talks straight out whether you agree or not. You know where he stands loud and clear. He makes it happen.

Politically, just once before I die, I'd like to see and hear a guy running for office say, "I don't stand for anything. My job is to represent the people in my district. Ask them where they stand. That's the most important thing on my political agenda. Not what the lobbyist and congressional friends want. My job is to represent the people who voted for me—not my stand on the vote. It's their stand that's important—not mine."

Now! I can just see my editor shaking her head. Bartos, this is June—not November. Write honeymoon, romance, marriage. Something like that in June!

Oh well! Tom Daschle stopping in Webster a couple of weeks ago brought back a lot of old memories. and it was big news in all the papers. He's a big wheel now. I'm sort of proud of him. But I'll have to admit, I never thought that skinny kid would go that far. But he had the makings—as the old-timers say—even back then.

I've seen him several times as he makes his yearly stops at Webster and area towns. It was two years ago at Pereboom's Cafe when he stopped by my booth. As I shook hands with him, I said, "You're sure getting skinny. Even your pants are too loose." "I've got to wear them out," he said. "I really haven't had time to get different ones. Bob Bartos," he said. "Haven't you got a son?" As I tried to answer, one of his aides grabbed his arm. "Tom, we're behind schedule." As he was being pulled away, he smiled and winked. "I'd like to talk to you more about that!" I knew and he knew we were remembering when he registered a Republican.

To Republicans, Tom Daschle is a pain in the butt. To Democrats he's their number one man. To me he'll always be that skinny Aberdeen kid who asked for my family's vote—and will always get it because I like the way he visited before and after he achieved his goals—to become a great congressman.

I'm sorry I missed him a couple of weeks ago. I should have been there—the fish weren't biting anyway. I was fishing, he was still working, and it wouldn't surprise me one bit if some day I might have to call that skinny Aberdeen kid Mr. President.

The birth of the Polka Dot Tavern

The most recognized and remembered building in Webster's Main Street history will be a 100-year-old condemned building known as Polka Dot Tavern. It was erected in the late 1880s by Charles Prior, a wooden frame two story building. Built on stilts, it was located in a slough hole now known as Polka Dot Park, on the corner of 6th Avenue and Main. It existed for 100 years until it was demolished in March of 1987.

In 1891 it was sold to John Severy, who leased it out as a cafe and rooming house upstairs. In 1910 it was known as Webster Cafe, operated by Frank Dickinson and Bill McKeown. In 1915 a woman operator, Mrs. Flemming took over, calling it Flemming Cafe, until selling it to E.P.Walker who named it Walker's Cafe. Sometime in the 1930s Walker built, remodeled and moved his cafe to the building now operated as the Decoy Bar. It was at this time John Severy sold the building to E.A. Locke and Andrew Hedman. It was rented to many operators, one was Andrew Hedman's brother, Olaf Hedman, Speed Queen washing machine sales. The rooms upstairs seemed to be always rented by the week and month.

In the mid-1940s Hedman and Locke sold the building to Olaf and Lars Sand, a couple of farm operators from the Langford-Pierpont area, who leased it out to a few 3.2 bar operators before taking over operation themselves. They called it the Sand Bar. With lack of upkeep and building repair, by the 1950s it had become an eyesore and was condemned as a fire hazard.

Rumor had it the bank across the street was waiting and pushing the city to tear it down so they could obtain the lot, at no cost, for their new bank building. Webster would welcome a new brick building on Main

Street. Ole and Lars Sand, weighing about 300 pounds each, were a couple of cracker jack characters, operating the bar in overalls. You either liked them or not. They had their own style of operating a business. Ole was one-third owner and two-thirds customer of the bar's 3.2 beer product line. Lars was two-thirds owner and manager. His bookkeeping system went something like this—bills to be paid in his back pocket, cash in his left pocket of his overalls. No paper work. But the Sand brothers wanted to go back to the farm. This city life of laws and paper work was not for them—they wanted out. But the bank would not buy a condemned building. They just wanted the lot it was on.

In 1954 my brother Frank, selling out his interest in a Seattle hotel, was coming home to Webster to raise his family. His motto—it only costs 10 percent more to go first class. everything he did, it seemed like, was more luck than talent. He could make any disaster into a happy happening. Breaking even was failure to him. He worked hard, played hard, enjoyed all the toys life had to offer and was a proud supporter of his family—being the best and having the best. Now Webster had an upcoming businessman to deal with—a hard worker.

Shocking everyone, in three day's time Frank checked out Main Street and the Sand Bar. Inspecting it, he made the Sand brothers an offer—they accepted at once. His first of many problems was about to start—with the bank, city, Sand brothers, all at once.

Ole and Lars said, "Give us the money, we will give you the key. But no paper work. No lawyers. And we are not signing anything. That just gets us into trouble." Well, you can't do business on Main Street that way. Abstracts, selling agreements, taxes and deeds had already given Lars and Ole a headache. Lars and Ole wanted out, Frank wanted to go to work. Finally a lawyer got it settled—he thought. When the selling price was to be paid Lars got 66 2/3 and Ole 33 1/3. Splitting that penny was something else. First, Ole couldn't understand why Lars was getting 67 cents and he only 33 cents. Lars was being overpaid and he wanted the deal legal—done right. Frank said, "OK, I'll give you 34 cents." Now Lars said he was giving Ole too much—it isn't legal. It took a few days of explaining before Frank became legal owner, and the Polka Dot Bar began in 1954.

Frank was now owner of a condemned eyesore building. Cleaning up the bar, meeting people, doing business, wrangling with the city and being harassed by the bank who wanted the location. The city wanted the building torn down and no improvements. The bank was happy he had problems.

Frank somehow got a permit to fill in the slough in back of the building on the grounds it would offer more city parking. The city didn't realize he would shore up the foundation of the condemned building at the same time. Next, inside work—no permit needed. Upstairs got new plumbing and wiring. He made it into a first class living quarters for his family—new windows, new carpeting—it was first class by anybody's standards. The bank across the street got more upset. Next, bar area improvements. The north side of the building was turned into a lounge-type area—jukebox, low lights, cushioned booths and, of all things, he carpeted the whole area. First in the state, others would follow, but Frank was the leader of carpeted floors for a bar.

Remember, this is a 3.2 joint—guys and gals from miles around meeting dates. It was a social gathering place of young and old alike. Gone were overalled bartenders, replaced with white shirts, neatness and clean. Gone were noisy drunks and rough language of the old operators. Gaining a reputation for the best hamburgers served anywhere was a sideline. Frank was running a first class operation inside. But outside was still an eyesore building. Wanting to remodel the outside, he tried to get a permit to build an office rental complex in back of the building. The city and powers that be—mostly the bank— had misjudged Frank's ability to make the business a success in the old building. It was rated by the health department the top rating for any bar in the state for a town this size, but somehow the condemned building remained an eyesore on the outside—a problem Frank could not solve. Fighting the city and bank, someone notified Frank that the state fire marshall was coming to condemn the building.

Next week, could Frank turn disaster into a happy ending? Polka dots are coming, after circles and dollar signs. The bank's mad, Frank's mad, the bar's doing great!

Polka Dot—from eyesore to star of Main

Frank Bartos, owner of a condemned building—Main Street eyesore on the outside with a first class updated inside could not get a permit to improve the shabby outside. The city, bank and powers that be were intent on removing this condemned building so the bank could put up a new brick building. The general public liked the place. Trying to get more evidence to bring the condemnation proceedings to closure, the state fire marshal was called to inspect the building. An unfavorable report could cause Frank to lose not only his investment, but his home and business. Almost giving up, Frank was exploring other business alternatives. Frustrated and angry, he was not about to give up. He was really upset—mostly with the bank across the street, who he thought was the root of all his problems.

The fire marshal arrived. He informed Frank he had talked to the state health inspector and was impressed with fine sanitation inspections he had received. Inspecting wiring, plumbing and foundation, which had been replaced, his report for the old building was not all that bad. Except for the outside. Of course a few free beers, Frank's wife's hamburgers—which the place was famous for—and homemade cookies didn't hurt either.

But Frank's repeated request to remodel the shabby outside was still denied. Painting was his only option. After gallons of linseed oil and two coats of white paint it looked only a little better. The bank was more upset. The banker told Frank that his building is condemned. "We don't care how much paint you put on it. It's going down, maybe with you in it." Frank retorted, "All you're interested in is getting something for nothing. You don't give a damn about improving Main Street or adding to it. All you can see is dollar signs coming your way." The banker was mad. "I'm so tired of looking out the office window at that eyesore. You'll be broke in a year anyway, wasting all that money on a condemned building." Frank may have made some returning remarks before he left, but I've told you enough of this clash!

Frank went back to the bar, got a can of black paint, went outside and started painting dollar signs and circling them all over the side of his newly-painted building facing the banker's office window. Frank and the banker were acting like a couple of kids instead of the men they were.

The general public never knew what the dollar signs meant. After one more clash with the banker, Frank stated, "That's my building—you'll never own it. If all I can do is paint it I'll paint it with polka dots. How would you like looking at that?" After hearing he couldn't do that, he did.

Getting five gallons of different paint, five brushes, making five cardboard circles, he and his customers started painting polka dots. Five polka dots painted got a free beer. It seemed everyone wanted to paint polka dots. Up on ladders, soon the building was covered. It drove the banker nuts with disgust. Can you imagine looking out your office window every day and seeing nothing but a wall of dizzying polka dots? Maybe the shabby wall of graying wood was better, but either way it was bad scenery.

What Frank had done in spite and frustration, he never in his wildest dreams imagined. He had created a lasting monument to the his-tory of Main Street. Not only the town, but the whole area was talking about the Polka Dot Bar. When traveling, telling someone you were from Webster, SD, the returning comment was, "Oh. The home of the polka dot building." The bar received nationwide attention in newspapers and magazines, write ups and pictures. Other places, Sioux Falls for example, would copycat the polka dot building, but the original will always be Webster's. Tourists would drive out of their way just to see or take pictures of the polka dot building. The condemned eyesore building on Webster's Main Street was now its star attraction.

Frank's painting polka dots to aggravate the banker was more luck than talent. One of Frank's traits had paid off—big.

Inside the Polka Dot business was also great. Young people for miles around were developing happy memories and friends that would remain with them the rest of their lives. Remembering their hosts—Frank, his wife and the bartenders— there are a thousand people both here and far away who, when hearing Polka Dot or Dot for short, it brings back happy times and memories.

Frank drowned in 1970 on a fishing trip. The old Polka Dot wept with the whole community. After a couple of good operators the Polka Dot was never the same. And in 1987, 38 years after being condemned, she was demolished.

I'm sure there's no beer in heaven, but whatever the saints and angels drink, God has a social gathering place. And Frank and the old Polka Dot are doing a thriving business and will leave a lasting impression on the whole world just as they have done on the Main Street history of Webster.

Best medical center west of Mayo Clinic

Horace Albert Peabody, MD, eye, ear, nose and throat specialist and druggist who loved the outdoors—lakes, hunting and wildlife, only second to family and his passion to serve people with his medical skills. In 1884 he was checking out the Webster area and decided this was the area to spend the rest of his life. He soon was joined by his oldest son, Dr. Percy D. Peabody, fresh out of medical residency at Mayo Clinic, and yet another son, Dr. Horace Claire Peabody. This family of doctors would form the nucleus of developing the biggest, best, updated medical center west of the Mayo Clinic—in Webster, SD.

First let's talk about Dr. H.A. Peabody—the father and first to arrive in Webster. It was his love of Pickerel Lake that was the final deciding factor to settle in Webster. In his travels to the lake he could shoot a dozen prairie chickens both ways, coming and going. He was one of the first to build a cabin at the lake. He was also the first Webster area man to own a gas machine car for travel, not as a toy. It was said he had a horse and buggy driver and mechanic on standby all the time because his 1903 Ford machine was always breaking down. If a rain shower came up he was stranded because no roads existed—just two track horse and buggy trails.An old reporter & Farmer paper quotes, "by 1905 Dr. H.A. Peabody had his second Ford car." He also was building a new home on north Main Street and several new cottages were being built at Pickerel Lake by local people. Dr. H.A. peabody had the first livable one. By 1907 Dr. H.A. Peabody had a car that could make the 23 mile trip to Pickerel Lake in one hour. That was going some with no roads, just buggy tracks across the hills.

In the same year Webster was classed as an automobile city, with 23 gas machine cars. Already Webster had an ordinance on parking and a speed limit of eight miles per hour. Offenders were being fined. A little later the speed limit was lowered to six miles an hour.

By 1910 Webster had four car dealerships— Buick, Ford, Overland and Rambler. Autos were selling at two a day and arriving at three or four train car loads a week. Webster auto sales serviced a 100 mile area.

Dr. H.A. Peabody, father of the Peabodys to follow, died March 9, 1911.

Now it was H.A.'s oldest son, Dr. Percy D. Peabody, with the help of his brother, Dr. Horace Claire Peabody who would take over the building of the Peabody Hospital and Clinic, with their inherent love of Pickerel Lake and the Webster area, their dedication of their lives to medical treatment of others. Webster was going to become the medical center of the northwest. First beyond the Mayo Clinic. Dr. P.D. Peabody Jr. would join the staff at a later date, making three generations of Peabody doctors.

In years that followed, Peabody Hospital would become an 88 bed unit—largest in the state, with a staff of eight doctors. A nursing school was established a block south across the street from the hospital (present day Steve Aldrich house) with the first Webster clay tennis court just south of the house, for the nurses' recreation and public use.

Most of the staff doctors were Mayo trained, some being called back to perform specialty operations. Art Lundquist, a blood analyst, an outstanding specialist, could analyze a blood sample in one hour, a marriage requirement that took other hospitals three days for results. Webster was known as the marriage capitol.

Back in 1919 Peabody Hospital was the only place in South Dakota equipped where a quantity of radium could be used in the treatment of any disease amenable to this new agent. Their x-ray equipment and the people who used it were ahead of all other facilities in the state.

It should be noted that the high standards of patient care were established with help of the Catholic sisters, continued by Anna Olsen, dean of the nursing school.

On the family side, who will ever forget Dr. Peabody's beautiful flower garden and cottage at Pickerel Lake? Full time gardner, Steve yrdanoff, flowers of all kinds, fish pond in the center full of fish and lily pads. That attracted visitors for miles around. Jess Riddle and Anna May Carlis are trying to repair and restore it somewhat to its original beauty. A lot of firsts can be attributed to the Peabodys. First oil heated home, sailboat, ice boat, motor launch, even the first fish shack with electric lights. Doc P.D. Peabody ran wires from his cabin across the ice to his shack for night ice fishing. When the doctors Peabody died, Webster lost a lot of firsts.

I never realized, and I feel Webster area people didn't either, what a legacy they left until I took my infant son to the Mayo Clinic in 1960. How great a staff of doctors Peabody Hospital had acquired! While going through the Mayo Clinic Museum, there in a large glass enclosed display was a shattered bone, wired together and a sign at the bottom explaining, this procedure developed by Dr. Walter P. Karlins, MD on staff at Peabody Hospital, Webster, SD. Going on, another glass case display, the sign at the bottom, this burn procedure developed by Navy Medical Officer Dr. Joseph Lovering, now on staff at Peabody Hospital, Webster, SD. Yet another by a Dr. Reid, whom I don't know. Dr. Dafin Lee was noted for some blood transfusion procedure by the Mayo Clinic. Some of this Peabody history is recorded, some not. It should be, other than in old newspaper clippings, where I found most of this column story.

I know in the 1930s, any kid who had a sore throat or earache ended up in the hospital getting his tonsils and adenoids removed. Or a mastoidectomy for an earache. I know myself and three brothers and most of my grade school had such operations. You seldom hear much of these operations now. Must be new medications used. And I will write this, more marriages were made in Webster and more babies born in Peabody Hospital in any three-year period than Webster can ever account for in the last 20-some years since Peabody Hospital ceased to exist.

9

What can we do about Dad—part one

Dad was a great guy—liked by everyone— loved by his family. At 80-plus years of age he was independent, talkative and fun loving. Sort of the life of the party type, but he didn't take directions. With all our love and concern—pleading, requesting, even nicely asking him—even his doctors telling him to cut down on red meat and eat more seafood, Dad joked, I see food, I eat it. Also saying, "If I had everything those doctors claim I have, I'd be quarantined." Changing his ways to stay healthy was a big joke. But to his family it was no joking matter. His over-active life style, gardening in the hot sun was almost unstoppable. His biggest joy in life was working in his garden, sometimes he rested, having a few beers with old buddies and friends. Early morning to late afternoon he was in his garden.

His garden plot covered the whole back yard. Like his younger neighbors, each fall manure was spread and a guy with a one-horse plow would plow and drag it. In the spring it was hand raked and twine was strung to keep the rows planted straight. Tomatoes and cabbage, planted in the house months earlier, were transplanted so he would be the first in the neighborhood to harvest. Dad even went so far as to start sweet corn in the house.

I would watch Dad make a mixture of green powder and water in a gallon can. He called it Paris green and flipped it on potato plants with an old piece of shingle to kill potato bugs. He dusted cabbage plants, thinned carrots, made ditches between rows with a hoe to run water down in the hot summertime, hilling potatoes, etc.

This garden was tough work and spending so much time out there at his age had to be stopped—he was getting nosebleeds. Doctors told him to stay out of the sun, out of the garden. Finally the doctors consulted the two sons and said that their dad could not work in the garden and could not consume more than 16 oz. of beer a day.

Watching the beer intake was no problem— these sons owned the two 3.2 beer bars in town— but keeping Dad out of the garden became one. The least amount of exertion would cause hemorrhaging and doctors couldn't control it. Talking did little good—he was out there picking beans and peas, digging early potatoes in the hot sun. Something had to be done to make him understand. One of the sons said, "The next time you go out in the hot sun and do garden work, we are going to have John Koenig dig a swimming pool where that garden is." Dad just laughed. The other son piped up, "That's a great idea. I'll go in with you—we'll split the cost 50/50."

Dad knew his sons didn't joke about doing things. If they wanted something they usually found a way to do it. Dad, a little concerned, said, "What a big mudhole that would be. Every kid in town tracking mud all over the place!" Well now! "Either you let us finish up your garden work or we'll dig it up and put in a swimming pool." This was Thursday night. Dad, calling our bluff as he left, "You two jokers wouldn't do that. You're all talk. I'm not worried one bit." The ball was in our court.

Friday John Koenig and his crew were going to load their heavy equipment on trailers—a cat pusher, backhoe, loader—for the move to Roslyn to start a ditch and sewer project.

Talking to our good friend about our problem with Dad, we asked if he could park his loaded equipment in the alley by the garden. Sure, he would go along with our scheme.

That afternoon the equipment was parked in the alley. Of course Dad wondered what was going on, but when one of the sons came across the garden where he was hoeing he heard the son talking to John, "You can start at that end about three feet deep and go to six feet at the other end," with John nodding his head, Dad had heard enough.

Out of the garden he went, headed straight downtown to tell his other son. Almost breathless, Dad explained, "That brother of yours is going to make the garden into a big mudhole, fill it with water from the fire hydrant and they are going to start digging in the morning. All the equipment is there, ready to go. You got to do something to stop him." Number one son, "Dad, remember, he told you—and the doctor told you to stay out of the garden—you laughed at them and us both." Dad interrupted, "Yeah! But I didn't think he would really turn it into a big mudhole."

"Swimming pool, Dad. You know you told my brother he couldn't build a big new home, well he did. You told him not to buy a big motor home, well he got one. You said carpeting a bar was unheard of, well he's got the first one in the state. When he says he's going to do something, I believe him. All he wanted was for you to stay out of the garden, for your own good, and the last resort was to make a swimming pool out of the garden." Dad again, "I never thought he would do it."

"Well, you come over for supper and we'll all sit down and talk about you staying out of the garden. Or do you want to play lifeguard for all the kids in the swimming pool?" "I'm too old for that!" Number one son, again, "You might not care, but we want you to stick around some more years. Remember, everything my brother does was taught by you. And he's pretty good at doing what he sets out to do. Maybe he's trying to tell you something—like stay out of the garden." Dad again, "I'll do anything to keep from having a mudhole in the back yard." "swimming pool, Dad."

Well, Dad had supper with his two sons and families that night. The wives would tend the garden. He promised to listen to the doctors, take his medicine and stay out of the garden. We knew Dad's word was good, so was ours. As monday arrived, John's ditching equipment left and the next year the back yard garden became a landscaped lawn with a young apple tree and Dad's old horseradish patch. And a few rhubarb plants—Dad's pie plants. But with time on his hands he spent more time with his old buddies and visiting old friends at his sons' bars. Knowing their schedules and with the 16 oz. limit, another problem developed. What it took to correct that is another column—next week.

What can we do about Dad—part two

Dad was 80-plus years old and enjoying life, under doctor's orders not to overexert himself and no more than two glasses of beer a day. The overexertion part we already took care of by eliminating the garden he had been addicted to. Now, with time on his hands, we had another problem. The two glass a day limit we had to deal with. The problem should have been easy to solve because his sons owned the only two 3.2 bars, Frank's Polka Dot on one corner, Bob's Bar on the other corner.

As I wrote before, Dad was a loveable old joker. The wives loved him, always fun to have around. The best babysitter, an errand boy, he was their buddy, always siding with them over his sons.

Two glasses of beer at one time would make him dizzy, but his old buddies were always slipping him that extra one. We tried everything. He wouldn't take directions from his doctors or us. to us this was a serious matter—we even tried blacklisting him for a week when we caught him cheating on beer intake. So he bought a pint at the city liquor store. One shot almost floored him and he hid it in the oven—he knew my wife would not allow hard liquor in the house.

As she was pre-heating the oven to bake a cake, there was a big bang! What a mess—stink and broken glass. Dad knew what happened. "Oh Francy, I'm so sorry! I must have forgot I put it in there!" Of course seeing how sorry Dad felt over the mess, she forgave him and laughed about it. But she would later tell me.

Consulting my brother about Dad's beer intake, the pint in the oven and about his health, he needed to follow doctor's directions. It was Frank who said "We've got to show him by example. Like we did with the garden." By saying we were going to make it into a swimming pool, and it worked.

Dad was a sharp old guy. You couldn't fool him easily—the plan had to work! It would be based on memory loss that he used as an excuse when he had two beers in the morning and sometimes three in the afternoon. When caught he would say, "I don't remember that—two this morning—or did I have one at two o'clock?"

At 9:30 a.m. Dad comes into the Polka Dot and there are both sons, Bob and Frank. "Dad, you're drinking too much beer. It's affecting your mind." "Yah, yah!" dad comments. "We're serious, Dad. You know what you did yesterday afternoon? You bought an old nag of a horse from a complete stranger. You gave him $10. Remember that? He said he would deliver it this afternoon. If he does, where are you going to keep that?" "You guys are crazy. I did not buy a horse!"

Jerry, my bartender was right there. Dad would believe him, but he was in on it and agreed that it had happened. Dad was now doubtful, but not convinced of his memory loss.

The plan had just begun. Doc Homer Caley, the vet, had just acquired an old freak sway-backed horse, which Frank had someone lead over to Dad's place while Dad was over at Bob's Bar talking with old buddies about memory loss, wondering if he had spent $10 for a horse.

Meanwhile, the horse was left tied to the clothesline post. When Dad got home the excitement began. The horse had already fertilized the ground, flies were gathering and Dad was wondering how it all happened. The plan went on.

Andrew Herrick, police chief and part of the plan, came by. He told Dad, "You know Jack, livestock and that horse are not allowed in the city limits. If you don't get it out of town I'll have to write you up." Dad said, "Please, please. I don't own this horse, you can have it. Just get it out of here!" "Jack, I'm afraid that's your problem. Why did you buy it in the first place?" "I don't know! I just got to get rid of it before it ruins the whole back yard." "Well, you better move it, Jack, or it will really cost you."

Dad headed right for Bob's Bar. Not for beer, but to tell his oldest son and ask for help. Not wanting to interfere with Frank's plan, my response to Dad's request for help was, "Look, Dad. The beer is your problem. It's causing all your troubles. You're ruining your mind. You can't remember—like the pint in the oven, buying that horse." "Oh! Bob, I'm really in trouble. Please get rid of the horse. Herrick, the chief, said he's going to fine me. My name will be in the paper and I've never broken a law in my life. You've got my word. No more beer unless you or Frank give me one, I promise. I don't have to drink beer! Please, I'll do anything the doctors say!"

Well, I believed Dad, but Frank was still not convinced. Before hid blood pressure got any higher, I told Frank to get the horse out of there—Dad had seen the light. In the meantime, Frank sent a guy over to Dad's place. This guy walks by Dad's house, saying, "That's a fine looking animal you got back there." Dad replied, "Think so? I'll give him to you. Take him." "No! I couldn't do that, but I'll buy him from you for $15." "Sold! I'll even take $10. Just get that horse out of here." Meanwhile, the guy paid Dad with a check, made out to Dad, signed, U.R. Stuck, so when Dad went to cash it it would be a lasting lesson and an example for him to consider. From memory loss of drinking too much beer.

Now, with the horse gone, Dad hurried to the Polka Dot Bar to tell everyone how he made $5 on the horse deal. He told Jerry, "Give all the boys a beer. I'll even have a short one myself—got to cut down, you know." Jerry took the check and gave him $13.50 in change. Frank came back to relieve Jerry for lunch, and found the U.R. Stuck check in the till. "How did this get in here, Jerry?" "The only check I took was from your dad, about a half hour ago."

It wasn't long before Frank was telling me I owed him $7.50—and the story of Dad cashing the check. We both roared with laughter, as did all our customers. Old Dad wasn't dead yet—his mind was sharp. I don't think he ever found out he cashed a no good check. Frank wasn't going to tell him, and neither was anyone else.

Dad was our pal and father. We wanted him to stay around forever. Of course, that was not to be. He peacefully left us at age 87 years.

11

Puppy therapy makes a person feel better

I've had a lot of dogs in my life—all great ones. But the one I miss the most is always the last one. And I clearly remember how the last one came about.

I was feeling great, laying in my hospital bed recovering from a cancer operation. Looking around the room full of flowers and the basket full of get-well cards by my bed, I felt for a moment like I was in a funeral parlor—and I might well have been if it wasn't for the outstanding doctors like Dr. Nelson and Likness and a great surgeon, Dr. Jim Larson. On and on my thoughts went—how my family missed my dad after he passed away. But Brownie, Dad's dog, missed him too. When he found Dad's old overshoes that he used to wear doing garden work, the dog gently picked them up, carried them out of the entry to the lawn, laid down beside them and quietly mourned. Why am I thinking like this? Must be the medication.

In came my wife. "Francis," I said, "No more flowers, bring me a puppy I can put under my bed. That would really cheer me up." "I can tell you're feeling a lot better," she said, changing the subject to something more realistic—like my hospital bill.

But I just couldn't get over wanting a puppy. After all, it was hunting season and I was going to do a lot more hunting. I needed a dog to ride in the pickup with me and chase down honkers and pheasants I was going to shoot. A puppy I could train—to love me, like Brownie loved Dad. Oh, sure I had a loving wife and kids, but the love of a dog is different. Waking to reality again, it must be the medication. The wife had gotten used to not having to vacuum up dog hair, replacing chewed up carpeting, replacing a couch, ruined by the dog. To say nothing of other messes. While enjoying the companionship of the dog, I remembered only the good times—my wife never forgot the bad. In fact, the dog we had became more attached to her than me. The dogs were somewhat like me—took orders, too—but we both got treats in the end.

"No more dogs. That's final." I remember her saying that to me. I was pushing my luck, just because I came out of the operation. She was babying me—but only to a point.

We were an hour early for my appointment with Dr. Larson for my check up. I asked if she would stop at the humane society dog kennel. "I just want to look. No dogs." Ok. We stopped. As I opened the door to go in, the smell hit us. The wife said, "I'll wait in the car. You go look." And I did. This one pen with about six black fur balls, one with a white spot on its chest, caught my eye. After all the wiggly jumping ones had licked my fingers, she just sort of ambled up to where I was kneeling and just looked at me. The kennel attendant said, "All these are from one litter, half springer, half lab. Are you interested or just looking? They won't be here long—we need the room." As I left to go, the pup with the white mark followed me to the end of the pen, while the others were busy eating. She even gave a little yip as I left.

After my next to last check up and final colonoscopy—Oh! that's a dilly!—Fran was feeling sorry for me. I said, "Let's stop at the kennel again. Her sorry for me part seemed to drift away. "No more dogs! You only look," as she let me out to visit the same pup.

Back home again, I couldn't forget the black pup with the white mark on her chest. And it wasn't the medication, as I was long off that. Finally, I started a conversation—if we had a dog it would be kept in the entry. It wouldn't come in the house. Her retort, "I know how long that would last. Every dog we've had has had the run of the house." "Well it's different now. I'm home all the time. I would train her and if I went to coffee or hunting the dog would go with me in the pickup. No trouble at all." My wife was listening but not softening her position on the matter, for a very good reason. This was my selfish want—not a need. The kids were all educated and gone. It was time for us to relax—not to accept another kid responsibility as this pup was sure to be. If we decided to travel and go places, then what? I was married long enough to realize that she was pretty much right most of the time.

It was my last checkup. I was in great shape. my last visit to this town, and last chance to visit my pup. My wife said, "I suppose, stop at that stinking kennel again?" "I would really like that. There in the kennel were only a couple of pups. No! My dog was gone! The pup with the white spot on her chest. Then behind me was the kennel attendant with my pup in his arms, the pup struggling to get to me. Putting the black pup in my arms, it licked my face and cuddled in my neck. The attendant again, "She's 12 weeks old today. Born Aug. 20." That's my birthday also. As I placed the pup back in the almost empty pen he went on, "the rest of the pups in this pen won't be here tomorrow. The vet will be giving them the needle tonight." I had a feeling about as low as when I was told I had cancer as I slowly walked to the office door to leave. There was my wife, even with the stink and smell she disliked, waiting for me. "Well, which one are we getting?" Running back to the pen, grabbing the black pup with the white spot on her chest, bringing her out in my arms, almost kissing my wife filling out the paperwork.

The pup slept in my lap all the way home, as my wife lectured me about the house rules for the pup. First she gets a bath, next a box and blanket in the entryway—and you better count on getting up tonight. She'll be yipping all night. And if she messes on the floor you better clean it up before I see it or back she goes. "No problem, I'll take care of everything." "Oh, sure you will," she said with sort of an insulting laugh.

Oh happy day! I had my dog—it was no dream, it wasn't the medication. I really had a puppy—training, watching her grow—the trouble we both got into. The smart and dumb things that puppy would do. I'll tell you all about it next week.

12

Josephine gets a name— JoJo for short

My newly acquired pup was home—her box in the entry—with the run of the house. Just like my wife had predicted, under her feet and following her all over the house. This three-month-old fat clumsy fur ball was something else. The ticking alarm clock in her box at night to keep her quiet had been removed. Now housebroken she was running all the time—never walking. She was clumsy and wobbled like a nervous old guy carrying a cup of hot coffee—slopping all over. And she had just grabbed hold of the bottom of my wife's flowing bathrobe. "Oh! You! You!" my wife yelled. That pup, clumsy as she was, whirled around, feet and tail flying and headed for the entry and her box. I knew better than to comment at this time—the pup and I both understood that tone of voice.

The pup had to have a name, not you, you. I wanted a name, something different. Not Blackie, Shep or Toby. She's a female, something my wife would come up with, like Josephine or something. But how would that sound in the field hunting with my buddies—hollering "Josephine" while they called manly names like Mac, Rex or Stud. How about Joe? Hey! Joe. I could call Josephine—JoJo for short. Not bad. In fact, a great name. My wife thought for once that I had a sensible idea for a dog's name. Josephine it was, but to me she would be JoJo.

Telling my buddy John Koenig that I named my dog JoJo he began laughing. "What?" I said, "JoJo is a good name." John, still laughing, said, "I know where you got that name from. Remember when we took that bear hunting trip out to Idaho? We stopped to have coffee and across the street there was a big sign and picture in front of a bar. Two scantly clad 350-lb. twin gals, Joann and Joan, called JoJo the gogo girls. Presenting tons of fun. Boy! How we laughed. "If it hadn't been 10 a.m. and we were running behind schedule to meet the rest of the group, we always sort of regretted not seeing that," John said, still laughing. (Boy is this column writer in trouble when Fran reads this!)

But remembering my friend John, laughing and loving my wife and dog too, the name was always important. JoJo the dog would now be part of the laughter and good times hunting.

JoJo became a smart good-looking dog. Always clean, no smell type, but lose hair, yes. The only place, other than the entry, she could go was beside my chair or in it. Fran could just look or nod and JoJo understood what she was supposed to do. In fact, out hunting pheasants she was all business. Her only fault was she would deliver shot birds to Fran, not to me. Even though I'd shot them, JoJo made it known she was Fran's protector, too. Feeling good about something, I grabbed Fran to give her a big hug. Up jumped JoJo growling and barking. Made me believe she meant business, too.

I never did train her to hunt. She did everything you would expect of a hunting dog. She saw geese and ducks coming before I did, laying flat on the ground no matter if it was doves, duck, honkers or pheasants. In the thickest of cattails or weeds she would find them. Leaving my blind to go to my brother Ed's blind (he had the coffee) a flock of geese was coming in when I was halfway there. Ed hollered, "Down! Geese!" I dropped to the ground, JoJo about 20 feet behind me did the same. When we got to Ed's blind after the geese flared off, Ed asked how I trained JoJo to do that. "I didn't train her. She just does things out hunting by herself."

I'd tell Fran I was going down for coffee, JoJo would perk up her ears and head for the door. She was a perfect pickup passenger, sitting erect in the front seat. Somehow she found the flasher button on the pickup. If I stayed too long having coffee the police chief, Ryan Peterson would say, "I turned your flashers off again." Then one day, he said, "Bartos, you can turn your own flashers off. That dog growled at me." JoJo became very protective of her pickup—and if I stayed too long at coffee, on came the flashers and I'd have to go. To the laughter of my coffee buddies. The dog was bossing me around.

One day, I opened the sock drawer. She ducked her head in and picked out a ball of my socks. I said, "Bring them over to the bed." From that day on, every morning she waited for me to open the sock drawer and she would pick out my socks. Fran also taught her to pick up my dirty socks by the bed and put them in the hamper. This was a daily happening.

In hunting season I would lay out my hunting clothes. If I didn't get out of bed right away when the alarm went off, here came JoJo with my hunting boots, throwing them down by the bed. And I better get up or she would bark and wake up Fran. Then we both would catch hell.

JoJo passed away about four years ago. Fran and I both sobbed. I know she'll never be forgotten. And I'm still hearing, "No more dogs." But I've been thinking of replacing JoJo with another fur ball pup. I may even take a trip to the humane society kennel—just to look! And I think Fran is about to let me do that—just to look! The house needs new carpet anyway. But I'm still hearing, "No more dogs. You're too old for another baby in this house."

And that's just what a pup is in this family.

13

Moon—an unforgettable horse

The year was 1948. Six guys—Herb Peterson, a filling and bulk gas dealer (where Thompson Oil is today); Oscar Ackerson, an implement dealer (located where Al's Plumbing building stands); Herb Ellig, manager of Thompson Lumber yard (now United Building Center); Ted Sveum, livestock trucker; myself and Rich Fiksdal—were meeting at Rich's store planning our big game hunt to Lewiston, MT, above Yellowstone Park in the Rocky Mountains. All of the guys were veterans of Strum's deer camp in the Black Hills. I was the youngest by 25 years—a real rookie. This was the last meeting the night before leaving. Everything was checked, packed and ready to go at 7 a.m. the next morning—one pickup and Rich's new 1948 Studebaker. Our overnight stop was a small town in Montana with slot machines all over the place. After supper Rich and I had a nightcap in a small bar. Feeling big time, after getting three silver dollars in change I put one in the slot machine. Clang, clang! I won $10! Before I could put the second dollar in, Rich put his hand on the machine and said, "Let that be the omen of the trip and let luck be with us."

Arriving at the ranch in early evening, all log cabins and a big log house, meeting and eating with the ranch hands who would be our guides for the next 10 days, we were informed all would be issued chaps and a horse for the two-day pack trip up the mountain, about 20 horses all together. We would reach the first base camp that afternoon and camp overnight in sleeping bags. All the time I felt the guides were sort of sizing up this group of new hunters. The one assigned to Rich and me didn't seem concerned about Rich—but he sort of wondered about me. Until he found out I was in the army. Then he let up on questions—about shooting and if I ever slept out in a sleeping bag.

At 6 the next morning horses were being saddled and assigned. I sure hoped I wouldn't get that spotted one they were having trouble putting a bridle on. Sure enough, I was youngest and lightest, so I got the wildest. The guides said, "He's a little tricky but he'll slow down after a couple hours on the climbing trail." The rest of the horses were the steady moving type.

I told Rich, "I think they named my horse Moon because that's how high he can buck a guy off." Just then I got hit in the back by Moon's head. Turning around, he snorted right in my face.

Everybody was giving their horses treats and petting them. I was so afraid of mine I thought he would bite my hand if I got too close to him. But for some reason he just kept putting his head in my back and pushing me. We were ready to saddle up. I knew this horse, Moon, was going to buck. Struggling to get up and seated, Moon never moved. He just turned his head and looked at me in disgust. We were in a single file column and I was sort of relaxing. All of a sudden I was on the ground. There was a fallen tree in the trail and all the other horses had just stepped over it. Not Moon. He made a quick sharp turn and went around it. While everyone laughed and Moon stood waiting for me as I struggled to get back up in the saddle, I swore Moon had a smile on his face.

Rich offered to trade horses with me, but I said I was beginning to understand Moon. He was tricky, that's all. But that afternoon I was about to find out relaxing in the saddle meant a rude awakening when riding Moon. All the horses had just walked across a small stream crossing our trail. Not Moon, he wasn't going to get his feet wet. He jumped it. He was on one side, I was sitting on the ground on the other. Then what did Moon do? He turned around and walked back through the stream he had just jumped, to where I was sitting on the ground and snorted right in my face. Standing waiting for me to get back up in the saddle, grabbing the saddle horn I was ready. Sure enough, he jumped it again—this time I stayed on.

Half hour to the first day base camp, the word was out. If we saw a young deer we should shoot it for camp meat. Rich was right behind me on the trail, when Moon stopped, turned sideways, his ears bent straight ahead, just staring. Rich said, "He sees something. Always look straight between where his ears are pointing." Standing a couple hundred yards out, four deer were looking at us. Rich told the others to keep moving, we were going to sneak back and get camp meat. He told me to shoot for the neck on a young deer, he would back me up.

We had our camp meat. We each had a hind quarter. Trying to tie my quarter on my horse, he went crazy. Finally, Rich took both quarters on his horse. Moon had stood on his hind legs and pawed the air with his front feet as I walked ahead, leading him. I was scared to get up in the saddle. He pushed his head in my back. Finally, I got nerve enough to get back up in the saddle as he stood still. He headed for base camp.

While guides made deer steak supper I unsaddled Moon. The wrangler guide put shackles on him so he could graze. "He's scared to death of wild game," the wrangler said, "but he's been real good today." "Yeah!" I said. "Tell my sore butt that." "Well, at least he didn't buck you off. You fell off." Enough said.

Sleeping bags all close together, the next morning I was awakened by a foul hot breath on my face. Looking up, there stood Moon, his two shackled feet next to my head. The wrangler in charge of horses asked, "How did that dumb horse step among all these sleeping bags without stepping on somebody?"

For the next 10 days I had a horse. No matter where I was, he was right behind me. Until the day I shot a black bear. He jumped and snorted and wouldn't go within a half block of the pack horse carrying it. The wrangler was getting worried about Moon and me. And being Rich and I had shot moose, elk and bear, he said maybe we could head back to the ranch ahead of the others. We could make it in one long day, he said, where it would take the rest and pack train two days. Giving us a trail map, next morning we took off. About midday snow storms hit us. The map was wet and the trail looked different. But not to Moon. He kept moving out. It was getting dark when we ran into the ranch fence—we made it. Unsaddling, watering and feeding our horses, as I headed for the ranch house, old Moon followed me. I held his head in my neck, and as I turned to leave he snorted at me—one last time. Two days later the rest of the crew arrived and we loaded the pickup and car and said goodbye. As we drove down the driveway, one spotted horse ran along the fence by the pickup.

I stopped and said goodbye again to a horse I'll never forget.

14

"I'm taking care of it for three days"

Old Bob had been driving by the kennel in the alley watching a litter of pups for six weeks. There was one black pup he had become very attached to. One by one the pups were being taken to new homes. Each day, sometimes twice, old Bob would drive by the kennel, stop and talk to the little black pup. The world's best dog, old Bob thought. If only he could convince grandma of that.

"No more dogs. That's final," was all he heard if he dared bring up the subject or even mentioned the pup that so reminded him of JoJo, who had been claimed by old age.

All old Bob could think of was training the pup. Oh! How great that would be. Dreaming of sitting on his stool in the rushes by the duck slough, his black lab waiting for the ducks. Bang, bang! Plop, splash. Out would go the pup, bringing back ducks. No more wading in knee-deep mud in waders. What a joy hunting would be again with the little black pup doing all the hard work. Just like it used to be with JoJo.

But grandma was more realistic. You're too old to raise a pup. A grown dog, maybe, but no pup. I won't put up with it. A pup is like a room full of two year olds—everything on the coffee table will be broken, hair all over the house, chewing up everything. No more pups. No more dogs. I've been there, done that! And besides, I'll get stuck with that dog. You'll be golfing, bowling, fishing. Then who's going to water, feed and take care of it? Remember the last time you tried to replace JoJo with a pup? It chewed the arm off the couch. That cost you! Remember that?

Now it was old Bob's turn. Grandma was so right, but old Bob would not give up. He knew this black pup would be different. It's so laid back. It will be in the fenced back yard, only allowed in the entry. Grandma again, "Yes, and it will howl all night just like all of them. And it won't be in the entry—it will have the run of the house just like all the rest. I don't need that. No more dogs. A pup is just like a baby. I'm too old for that kind of responsibility and so are you!"

It was the Fourth of July when old Bob drove up the alley to the dog kennel to look at his black pup again. It was empty! The mother was there, but all the pups gone.

Then the nice young fellow who owned the pups came out of the house. "Did someone get that little black female pup?" old Bob asked. The young guy smiled. "No, I think that pup belongs to you. I put her in the shed. Some guys are coming over to look and I knew you would be coming by looking, like you have been for weeks."

As he opened the shed, out came my pup. Picking her up, she licked my face and I knew we both were in trouble with grandma as I put her on the seat beside me in the pickup.

I put her in my fenced back yard, got puppy food and water, borrowed an old doghouse. The pup was very happy. Then grandma noticed it. "What's that dog doing in our yard?" "I'm taking care of it for three days—while the guy's going on vacation," old Bob lied!

That pup sure was a charmer as it came up to grandma and sat looking at her—not even jumping up like most pups do. Grandma said, "You better bring that pup inside. It's too hot out here for that black pup. In the entry! I won't have her running all over the house."

Soon the neighbors noticed. "What a good looking pup. I've got a plastic kennel you can borrow if you're going to keep her inside." "What's her name?" Grandma said she looks like pepper, all black.

Now old Bob had a name. "Come on, Pepper," he said. Grandma's motherly instincts took over. She put a rug in the plastic kennel and began talking to the baby pup. Old Bob never said a word. The pup was doing more charming than old Bob ever could.

"Just wait. Tonight that pup will be howling all hours," grandma said. "You'll be up all night. You'll be glad to take her back." Surprise! The pup never made a sound. Slept all night. Even grandma commented on that. So far, so good!

Problem #1—Old Bob, just like grandma said, was scheduled to play in a two-day golf tourney with the young guys. And that pup had to be closely looked after. Grandma had already said she would put glue on the golf cart seat and put that pup on it. She was not going to take care of it. It was old Bob's problem to care for and feed that pup.

At 6 a.m. he took off with his foursome to play golf some 50 miles away, leaving that pup with grandma in charge. Without her knowledge or consent.

Arriving home that night, not knowing for sure what to expect, another surprise. There was that black pup following every move grandma made in the kitchen. In fact, she was even carrying on a conversation with the pup. "Good girl," she said, as she patted the pup.

Old Bob said, "I'll be taking her back tomorrow. She'll be out of your way. I think you're right. Pups are like little kids turned loose in a room full of knickknacks. You're getting too old to put up with that." "Whoa!" grandma said. I'm not that old. And every once in a while we end up with a two year old who's a perfect lady, just like this pup. All I've heard is dog, dog, dog for the last six months. Now we've got a good one and we're keeping her!"

Oh happy day! Old Bob had his pup. Grandma made that quite clear. She was going to be part of the family. Old Bob settled into his easy chair, Pepper on the rug beside him. Not to be outdone in the charm department, he commented to the pup, "I've sure got a history of picking good looking females. After all, I picked grandma out over 55 years ago—and I did a good job of that!"

"Quit talking like that, you old fool!" she retorted from the kitchen.

If it becomes a fact or not, old Bob is dreaming of sitting on his stool in the rushes going bang! bang! at the ducks. And when one falls his black pup will do all the hard work, splashing to get the duck while old Bob enjoys the hunt with his dog.

And grandma enjoys her black shadow following her around the house the rest of the year. Dogs are truly a family affair.

15

Official downtown weather from Bob's Bar

It was in the late 1950s when Webster businessmen started to realize that the declining farm population in Day County could no longer support Webster's Main Street businesses; and they better start promoting Webster to draw outside industry if the town was to survive. One of the first ideas to get Webster noticed and outside publicity was "Webster, Petunia Capitol of the World." It got going about 1961 and was in full swing in 1967 when a disc jockey from watertown's KSDR radio station called me and said he was starting a half hour weather program. He would call surrounding towns and get weather information. Webster's time slot was 8:45 a.m. monday through Friday. I recommended myself, since I bought the Peabody duplex and a weather station was there. I moved it to Main Street in front of my bar—all it amounted to was a mercury temperature gauge that recorded high and low for 24 hours. Preparing for my weather report I needed road conditions in the area. This I figured I could get from early morning bread delivery trucks from Watertown and Aberdeen and the Hyman freight truck driver coming in from the east, as the freight house was located only one block from my bar on Main Street. Wind speed was determined by the flag up the street by the post office. Limp flag—4.5 mile per hour wind; half blowing flag—12.4 mph; flag straight out—15-20 mph. An old sergeant once told me, "Never answer any officer in about five miles. When asked a question say '5.3 miles per hour, sir!' and they will assume you know what you're talking about." So if I was going to be a weatherman I would give wind speed at 6.4 miles per hour and so forth.

Webster needed publicity and so did Bob's Bar. And it cost nothing except my time—the phone call was their nickel. I would have about 10 minutes, but one thing for sure, I was going to get in big trouble (unbeknownst to me at the time).

I'm sure there are readers who remember Webster's weather reports from Bob's Bar. They ran for almost three years—until I sold the bar. The program became more of a comedy than a report—even though it was somewhat factual— and I understand it had a great following of listeners. Here's an example. "Howdy! From the petunia capitol of the world, Webster, SD. It's a beautiful March day in downtown Main Street. Our wind is 6.4 miles an hour out of the southeast, temperature is 22.3 degrees above zero, our overnight low 12.6 degrees and the high today will reach 31.3 degrees. And let me add, yesterday's comments by Sisseton mayor Al Krommer, that Sisseton is now known as the pan fish capitol of the world. Well, all I got to say is Webster's fishermen use his pan fish for bait in our area." On cold days we used comments like "It's so cold this morning it was freezing nuts and bolts right off the gang plows," and "saw two cottontails pushing a jack rabbit to get him started." Of course other weather reporters from other towns made comments. It became a fun hour program.

Until one day I made the broadcast saying official downtown petunia capitol of the world— Main Street temperature—wind speeds, etc. A few days later a guy in a black suit, white shirt and tie came into the bar wanting to talk to the man making the broadcast. Thinking, "Boy, I've hit big-time listeners now!" I proudly said, "I do." Where upon he pulled out a big leather billfold with a badge and picture on it, saying "I'm with the department of interior. You've been giving official US government weather reports over the air waves and Day County has an official weather observer. He's responsible for weather reports. Your broadcast will end as of now and no further action on our part will be taken. And, by the way, I would like to see your wind gauge that can show wind speed in tenths of a mile per hour when the federal station at Aberdeen records only to the nearest five miles per hour." Now, scared stiff, I took him outside and pointed to the post office flag. He just shook his head and left, as I ran to lawyer Bill Holland's office. Breathless, I told him what happened. As he told me to settle down, he said, "I listen to your program and I've never heard you say United States or government. You always say official downtown Webster or official petunia capitol of world downtown temperature. The Day County weather recorder is half mile from your bar. Temperature and wind speeds vary. Give me that dictionary. Official is an adjective. You can use it all you want if you don't put government behind it. You've got every right to say official Main Street or official petunia capitol of the world. If that guy shows up again, you bring him up here to me."

Well, I kept on broadcasting and no one ever showed up to stop me again. My lawyer's advice cost me $10 of Bill Holland's time.

Right today it's hard to talk county or city personnel into reporting the weather—or just temperature to the TV stations. There's a big blank spot on the screen between Watertown and Aberdeen that TV stations would gladly fill with the name, Webster, if someone had the leadership to direct a person to call on their 800 number. The time, cost is nothing— publicity for Day County and Webster, the county seat, great exposure at 6 and 10 p.m. Even the sheriff's weather station equipment is free from the department of interior to not only the county and city. Just check into it—a five-minute job worth hundreds of dollars worth of publicity for the area—is being wasted.

16

A chicken in every pot—except ours

Even in the late 1930s it wasn't uncommon for small town citizens to have chicken coops in the backyard. Sunday chicken dinners and daily egg breakfasts were a regular menu of most households—or so it was at our house. scrambled, poached, fried, hard-boiled, egg salad—you name it, we ate them all as a main staple of our meals. Beyond breakfast.

The main mode of freight was train, not semi trucks as today—for both perishable and canned goods. But the most perishable of all, around Easter time each year, was baby chicks. The railroad depot became a chirping mess, with flat boxes with round vent holes full of six-day-old baby chicks farmers had ordered from catalogs. They were yellow fuzzballs with names on the outside of the boxes. Like Rhode Island reds, white giants, Leghorn, Plymouth Rocks, black giants and others. Some even contained peeping ducks. It was a depot agent's nightmare—the peeping and chirping in the warm depot. The freight house was just too cold for the baby chicks, in desperate need of food and water—having spent a third of their life in baggage car travel. It was also a time when the area got hit with a big snow storm, blocking roads to travel. About like the present day class "B" basketball tourney weather almost every year in South Dakota. Only in those days no 4X4 pickups. No big snow plows. Just getting something started or a path to the barn was a problem for farmers. And here sat the poor depot agent with all these boxed hungry and thirsty peeping baby chicks. Most would be picked up and delivered by the end of the day—but there were always a couple boxes left. Survival rate was about 50 percent 24 hours after arrival at the depot.

The depot was my loafing place—because my dad worked for the railroad and I could make a nickel delivering Western Union telegrams. John Lockwood was a friendly depot agent, also.

Now after 16 hours, a four box shipment of chicks—12 dozen, three dozen to a box—yellow fuzzball chicks were on the critical list, the snowstorm getting worse. When my dad arrived at the depot to report, the signal outage had been repaired and the line cleared. The agent asked my dad, "Jack, got any place for 12 dozen chicks?" My dad said no, but I said, "Couldn't we put them in the wash house? Mother washed clothes today—it's warm in there. All they need is food and water." John Lockwood, again to my dad, "They are all yours, Jack. If you take them you'll be doing me a favor. They'll all die anyway if they don't get out of these boxes and get watered and fed."

"Go ask your mother," Dad said. Home I ran, telling Mother, who seemed as excited as I was. "Sure we'll take them for nothing!" Telling my brothers she needed cardboard boxes to line the wash house floor, "When are you bringing them home?" "Right now!" I said, as I left for the depot to tell Dad.

With the depot agent carrying one box, Dad carrying two and me one, we made the one-block trip to our house. Out in the wash house Mother was the general. My brothers had gotten boxes from Red Owl and the Elevator Store. The floor was lined with cardboard, pie tins were full of warm water. She was boiling eggs to be crumbled for chick feed. Dad was directed to the Equity Elevator to get cracked wheat and bran from Ike Overton, the manager. Mrs. Dupree from next door came over saying Henry, her husband, was getting a brooder hood out of the barn to bring over and Dad should wire the light to it. Also, Mother was directing him to bank the stove with coal.

The boxes were opened. About 100 yellow fuzz balls came out— about two dozen had died—some were wobbly. The floor was covered with them. My mother and us kids were excited as the chicks crowded the pie tins filled with food and water.

Mother would be up most of the night tending her flock—only losing four or five during the night. The rest seemed very healthy.

Mother's laying hens were in the barn out back. We also had an old brooder house full of junk that was used for storage, and Mother needed her wash house back to wash clothes. The chicks would have to go in the brooder house.

We all got busy moving out junk and cleaning the brooder house. For heat, Dad got hold of an old wick burning kerosene upright round stove. In the next few days the brooder house was lined with cardboard. Everything appeared cozy. The chicks were doing great and Mother had her wash house back.

No one at the time realized we had created a big problem—a kerosene round wicked heater, no chimney and we had made the place almost air tight for warmth.

It was about 2 p.m. when I was called from class and told by Mr. Herb Hartshorn I was needed at home—at once. When I got there the fire department was putting water on the smoldering remains of our brooder house. The kerosene stove had blown up from lack of outside air. All that remained of the chicks and brooder house were wet ashes.

I think that was the first tragedy I had really witnessed in my life. But we all got over it and were extra nice to Mother, who felt the greatest loss. Dad said, "Don't worry, I ordered some six-week old springers from Joe Valentine (a farmer friend). We'll get them when it warms up." Dad also got Gus Cantop's team and wagon to load up the ashes and cleaned up the mess. And the family carried on—spending time looking at the Yankton Gurney seed catalog. Spring was coming. Mother was busy growing tomato and cabbage plants in all the windows facing south in our house for the big garden we would soon be planting.

In those days everyone seemed happy with what we were going to do—and content with what we had. Instead of remembering what could have been.

Christmas in the good old days

At Christmastime people get "Santa-mental" so to speak. With snow falling and wind blowing outside, I sit in my big easy chair and start recalling Christmases past. What an exciting time! Better than the Fourth of July, I think. christmas lasted for almost two weeks at our house. In our neighborhood, one block off Main Street, one block from the railroad tracks, 70 years ago, my family was an average example of the times in our section of town. This is how it was.

Dad had a job on the railroad, Mother was a part-time cook at a cafe and full-time mother of five boys age eight down to one and a half-year-old Donny.

In 1930 no one knew the meaning of poor. Everyone existed, content to live by what they earned and hoping tomorrow would be better. We considered our family average. We had a house, Dad had a job and Mother could make great meals without spending money on store bought stuff. We had a big summer garden and cellar full of canned goods. Everyone had a chicken coop and even hogs and cows. And yes, our neighborhood was a block off Main.

Two weeks before Christmas, Dad brought home an evergreen he cut along the railroad tracks. Out of an old wooden box he made a stand. Then the fun began. Dad gathered about 10 discarded railroad cross arm poles and traded them to a farmer for a peck of field raised popcorn, which Mother would pop in an old cast iron frying pan. While us kids would string popcorn with thread and needle to decorate the tree Mom would make popcorn balls and Dad would dig out steel clips to hold half-burned candles from last year. They would be lit on Christmas Eve. Later, starched handmade doilies like snowflakes, stars and angels were added—and a big cardboard star on the top. I can't recall any outside decorations on any houses in our neighborhood.

Then there were the expenses. Mother tried to round up two cents for each of her five boys to go to the church Christmas program. everything clean, patched and pressed, clothes mostly too big or small, Dad trying to polish worn out shoes, finally off we went. Pulling Donny in the sled, singing songs like "Jesus Loves Me" and "Hail, Hail the Gang's All Here—What the Hell Do We Care" at the top of our voices, not knowing the meaning of the words. The church program was great—a sack of candy and an apple, what a great deal. Putting our two cents in the collection plate we felt like rich bigshots.

Christmas Eve there was oyster stew for Dad and Mother, cocoa, chocolate pudding and pancakes. Sounds strange, but that's what christmas Eve was. The tree with candles lit for only a short time—Santa was coming tonight and we had been oh! so good! Nothing was under the tree. Santa Claus always brought gifts during the night—if we were good. Otherwise all you would get was a stick and a piece of coal. That was a well-known fact—it never happened at our house.

What was considered being good? All kids had chores to do—this was expected. Like carrying out ashes, shoveling a path to the chicken coop and barn. We had 20 laying hens and a mean old rooster. We picked eggs, fed and watered them, kept the coal bucket full and kindling wood piled in the entry. Also our job was pumping cistern water to fill the reservoir on the kitchen stove and on washday fill the boiler and tubs with soft water which Mother would use, after washing clothes, to scrub and clean the outside privy. What a cool trip to the toilet in the daytime. And of course we had a chamber pot with a lid at night. Another chore for us to take care of dumping and cleaning that.

Our presents to Dad—going up and down the alley in back of stores, picking up cardboard boxes and wooden crates, filling big boxes full so Dad would have a fire starter for the kitchen stove for a month or so. For Mother—old Ike Overton, grain elevator manager let us sweep up the spilled grain. In a 10-day period of being pests there we got enough to winter Mother's 20 laying hens to spring.

Christmas morning! Oh happy day! Home-made gifts crafted out of wood, new painted wooden sled, sling shot, rubber gun with a clothes pin trigger, thread spool made with a rubber band and match stick that when wound up would run across the floor. And even store-bought striped overalls—big so we could grow into them.

Soon it was dinner time. Stewed chicken and dumplings, best ever. (Two or three days later we would find out the mean old rooster was gone.) That was another unexpected present. Egg picking would be a lot easier and safer now. Oh! the hand cranking of the ice cream maker. Mother had traded a dozen eggs to Gus Cantop for a tin pail of cream. The man had three cows and 20 acres of land two blocks west of our house, an area filled with residential homes now. Then warm mincemeat pie. Christmas Day was great!

By today's standards it's hard to believe a sane man could have such happy memories of a bleak 1930 Christmas, but everyone was equal in our neighborhood. We didn't know better things in life existed. Our biggest reward in life, at suppertime when mother would say to dad, "Did you see all the wood the boys piled in the entry?", or "The boys did a good job cleaning the chicken coop."

I enjoy a great Christmas with my family each year. But I will always have great memories of my kid years—with my four brothers in the early dirty 30s. Maybe it's because they have all passed away and we can no longer be together. One thing is for sure, I wouldn't be able to enjoy it today—now that the modern world has changed my lifestyle. I wonder if some writer in 2070 will write his memories of Christmas 2000 and feel as old fashioned as I do right now. And like me, no one will ever be capable of bankrupting our great memories of the past.

18

Freedom and rights are earned, not given

It was Tuesday, Sept. 11 about 9:25 a.m. that I saw the hijacked terrorist planes hit the World Trade Towers in New York on television. I—like everyone else—was shocked, with fierce anger. After a half day of watching I turned it off. After hearing remarks that it was worse than Pearl Harbor, my mind went back 60 years, like it was yesterday.

As an old WWII vet I recalled the attack on Pearl Harbor and how I was informed about it without TV. It was 1 p.m. Sunday, Dec. 7, 1941. Along with other kids, I was reporting to basketball practice in the old Webster High School gym. As I arrived Coach Welch had the radio on in his coach's room. He called us all into the room. "Boys," he said, "There will be no practice." With tears in his eyes he said, "You'll all be soldiers in less than a year. Some of you will die. That's your future—protecting this country. This is serious." As kids we were shocked at our coach, who was always giving us pep talks. Having him talk to us like that, with tears flowing, you could hear a pin drop. It was silent as we listened to the news and radio reports. America under attack.

The coach was right! Most of the class of 1940-1943 ended up in service of their country. Even before our class graduated in 1942 a teacher and five or six of our high school classmates were killed. Lots more would be killed and wounded in the next three and one-half years of combat. It was true for 15-17 year old kids of the 1940s as it is today. Only our enemy was clear cut—Japan and Germany. Today the enemy is faceless, but just as evil.

Preventing an illness is a lot easier than curing one. And American has the burden of curing a terrorist evil now.

We have been very lax in preventing, by letting our patriotic Americanism be undermined. First of all, you shouldn't expect to have freedom until you earn it. Too many people have entered this country thinking, "I'm American. I've got my rights. The land of the free," before they even understand our rules and laws that make us Americans.

They make no effort to learn American English, even though we provide schools for them. Instead they expect us to educate their children in a foreign language. It appears the first thing after entering our country they learn is "my rights." Well now, you shouldn't have rights until you earn them and are willing to shed your blood and lose your life for American freedom. Just like WWI and WWII guys did, even against the countries they came from. Americanism isn't cheap. A lot of us have paid the price.

And when some young person tells his parents, teacher or cop, "I've got my rights," he should be straightened out at once. Because without a job, without paying taxes or being a great asset to his community he hasn't earned any rights. Not until he obeys the rules this democracy was established on. Like our freedom, rights are not given. They are earned. Majority rules, not minorities.

Who interpreted our laws? Saying schools couldn't use a few minutes to respect the American flag or say a prayer of their choice? Or a court system that allows a minority of people to burn our American flag in a public protest, while the majority of us burn in anger.

In the 1980s I visited Iowa State College. I'm sure there were others, but this I can confirm. Iranian students were passing out pamphlets processed on their class computers condemning the shah of Iran, a leader who had an American born wife and was leading his country to a democratic form of government. These students were chanting in groups, "Down with the shah" and almost forcing American students to take their printed propaganda. Asking a student why he even took a pamphlet, he said that by placing it on the outside of books he was carrying they didn't harass him. A state-supported American college was taking foreign students, letting them have prime time classes in computers and technology while American kids had to schedule late night and early morning hours for high tech and computer classes. This raised my American anger but no one was very impressed with one person's objections. It was soon forgotten.

Visiting the union building and cafeteria, which should have been filled with American kids, it appeared to be the hangout of Iranian students. I felt like I was in a foreign country instead of an American college.

It was only months later the shah of Iran was replaced by a leader who held our embassy hostage. One hundred fifty some American prisoners with some Americans dying trying to save them. Somehow this was soon forgotten and there were a dozen other terrorist training places, including our own armed forces, for terrorists.

Too many of the eagles' tail feathers have been pulled by terrorists. Now it's time for those terrorists to feel the sharp claws and beak of that American eagle as its friendly world kindness turns to patriotic American anger. Which means war on world terrorism and evil. Our lives and standard of free living will change only until the war is over. Like a big boil on our butt, it will get worse before it gets better.

Sept. 11, 2001, somewhat like Dec. 7, 1941. Our freedoms will be restricted, but will never disappear. Our wants will temporarily be reduced to our needs.

Pearl Harbor produced the greatest generation. Maybe this attack will produce a greater one and an even better America than the great one in which we live today.

19

Qualifying for the greatest generation

A lot of my old buddies are talking about South Dakota's honoring WWII vets with a memorial to be dedicated in Pierre Sept. 15. I'm sure you'll be reading and hearing speeches about the greatest generation. I'm also hearing a lot of young guys in their 60s referring to themselves as part of the greatest generation.

Well now, other than being 70 plus years old and a WWII vet, it appears nobody has set any solid guidelines or criteria for what qualifies you to be a member of the greatest generation. Of course, if you worked through WWII, spent time in the dirty 30s and are 70 plus years old there's no doubt—you're a charter member of South Dakota's greatest generation. So my buddies and I have established a few guidelines we think qualify people to be part of South Dakota's greatest generation. Here's our list.

1. As a kid your daily chores included piling wood, filling the coal pail and carrying out the ashes from the wood and coal burning kitchen stove, filling the stove's hot water reservoir from the rain barrel, if you carried a lantern to the barn and milked by hand, and if you ever found the barn was as good a place for you to use as a toilet—better than the cold outhouse privy—you qualify as part of the greatest generation.

2. If you can remember trapping, snaring and drowning out flicker tails and striped gophers, then saving their tails in a Prince Albert tobacco can or trapping muskrats and mink before and after grade school for clothing money, or when a job for room and board was more important than going to high school, or if you remember going to the outside privy in -10° winter weather, sitting on frost covered nail heads that caused frost burns and scars on your butt, but also felt the pleasure of peach

wrapping tissues in canning season—that replaced rough catalog paper—that may make you a member of the greatest generation.

3. Living in the depression era of the dirty 30s, eating food was like chewing rough sandpaper. Dust storms and dirt flying everywhere, grass hoppers so thick they blocked out the sun. Doors and windows had to be closed with rags under the window sills and doors to keep dust and dirt out. It was so hot and everything gritty. No one had fans, only fans you waved by hand—no electricity. Wells went dry, water was hauled in by a horse-drawn wooden tank wagon and stored in a cistern, which usually held some frogs and lizards. And if you got a tin pail of milk it tasted like the weeds and Russian thistle cows were eating to stay alive. And it was a common fact the cows got really loose on a diet of dirt, weeds and this-tles. Even standing 10-15 feet in back of them you were in the danger zone of being sprayed. Or if you ever licked the frost off a pump handle and your tongue stuck to it. Yes, if you experienced that era you're part of South Dakota's greatest generation.

4. Now, let me tell you about the South Dakota WWII vets serving in the armed forces until 1945. For most it was their first time out of South Dakota, finding out army hours of 5:30 a.m.-4:30 p.m. and getting Saturday afternoon and Sunday off was less working hours than they had back home. Being issued the best clothes they ever owned, finding out underwear came in two pieces rather than long johns was something new! Also taking a shower daily compared to the once a week washtub baths was a thrill. Trying to understand the big-time talk of New York and New Jersey guys, also the southern guys and Texas guys talked dif-ferent. Being called a Dakota hayseed didn't last long in many outfits. Because of our hard working and physical makeup they soon gained the army units' respect—on the rifle range as sharp shooters, tank drivers, pilots and squad leaders. Their reputation soon spread throughout the armed forces. For all that followed, South Dakota produced the best sol-diers.

5. The greatest generation will soon be history of the past and so called youngsters of today, baby boomers in their 50s and 60s will be writing their history to the people. In a few years, their so-called hard-ships and life, to a generation of kids in the 2000 era. And I'm sure they will find the same disbelief of their history as younger people find in my remembering!

I can just imagine writing about things that happen in the 1960s to a kid born in the 2000 era. It goes something like this:

1. In school we had to do all our research and homework from books. No computers. We had to add and subtract math problems without a calculator.

2. We had a teacher for every 15 students in the room, explaining our lessons in history in a novice way compared to the expert TV professor they will be using tomorrow—with no teacher.

3. Writing will become a lost art, as will letter writing in long hand. E-mail and computers will be the communications of the future.

4. What goes around comes around. And like us 75 plus year old guys talking about the greatest generation, you'll have your honored past also. Maybe greater than the one we are going to celebrate. But I do hope you don't have to go through wars and the great struggle we did. But you already have your Vietnam, Gulf War and a few other history making incidents that will be hard to explain to future generations.

One thing about going through and living history, you never realize it's happening. It's just daily living and routine. Then, years later, you read how bad it was or how great it was. That's history. And you can say "I lived it."

Back to the daily routine of life—for now

President Bush said America is at war. He doesn't want this great country to give in to terrorists and wants citizens to resume their daily routines as soon as possible.

After us old retired guys got over our anger, shock and flying our flags at half staff, half mast for Navy vets, we took our Commander-in-Chief at his word and order. To get back to our daily routine of life.

Knowing us old guys, regardless of where we live—city, farm, small town—we are somewhat alike in our thinking and actions. We are proud of what we have done in our lives, the way we dealt with past attacks on American freedom—Pearl Harbor, Korea and Vietnam—that we have fought for, lived through and basically solved.

Most of us old guys don't fully understand the changes in this high tech world we live in today. We think of ourselves as top dogs in a slower paced world and are slow to adapt to fast changes. We are very proud of our kids on the inside. On the outside we can't understand why they make more money in one year than we retired on. Or why they buy a car and pay twice the price of what we did for the home we live in. Nor do we fully understand this new faceless enemy that has attacked our country.

The best thing us old guys can do, after bragging we laid the foundation for this younger generation who will deal with this enemy is to stay out of their way and not become a burden to them. Oh yes! We can cheerlead and help in ways we can support them when they direct us to. Otherwise let them do their own thing and our freedom will be safe.

Us WWII vets talked about early 1943 in London, long before D-Day of the English home guard. Most 75 year olds plus, WWI English vets, acted as air raid wardens and firefighters proudly directing rescue efforts and fighting fires among blocks of rubble during night and day bombings. Buzz bombs, rocket attacks to save victims and their homeland. Because us old guys have enjoyed the American good life and freedoms longer than the younger generation we have a strong patriotic spirit to protect it. And any enemy who thinks he can pick the fruits of freedom from the American tree of life is dead wrong.

Enough of the past, let's talk present. Obeying President Bush's order—to resume our daily lives and routines. In the case of us old guys, our daily routine usually starts at the local cafe with coffee talk. One guy complains the coffee is too weak or too strong. They just don't make coffee like they used to. Best coffee is when grounds are mixed with an egg in a big pot. No filters. Like the rural church ladies aid makes. And look at those plastic things with that imitation white stuff they call cream. No wonder we don't have milk cows on the farm anymore. Another guy starts on government policies, cussing and discussing politicians. Democrats, Republicans and anyone else he can think of. Of course the young waitress handles the coffee complainer with some wisecrack, stating he should join the 21st century. We are all sure anyone can join with comments for or against the government without any fear of some guard sticking a bayonet in our back and marching us off to jail. We have earned the right of free speech and are sure our younger generation will see that we keep it. Not always expressing our feelings on the outside but on the inside we are proud and very thankful.

I hope no one judges the old guys by the way we express ourselves. Let me give you a personal example. As I arrived home doing the daily routine the mailman handed me the mail. Outwardly I bitched about the big electric bill. Inside I felt good because my house was warm in the winter, cool in the summer. No black sooty stovepipes to clean. No ashes to haul out, no coal pail to fill, no wood to chop. Life's great—not like the old days.

As I stood by the mailbox, back came the mailman. "I forgot one," he said. It was my last half tax notice. I got mad all over again, cussing the county commissioners, mayor, school. Again, on the inside I felt good. I had budgeted for this, I could pay it and I felt good. I had earned my pension, my social security. As I stuck out my 79 year old chest, I was proud of myself. I'm a taxpayer, an asset to the community. And besides, I still would have a dollar left for coffee and tip for the wisecracking waitress tomorrow.

Entering the house, my wife of 56 years (how can I say this) requested emphatically that I mow the lawn, clean the eaves and get something done besides golf, hunting and having coffee again. Sudden gloom set in, but I knew better than to express myself too much.

Again, while doing these chores, my spirit was given a lift. I own this house and how lucky I am to do these things. I felt so good I thought I'd go in the house and give my wife a hug. Maybe just a kiss will do it. America—a great place for old guys to live. About seven out of 10 Americans own their own homes. Less than one out of 200 in the world can say that.

Next morning, 6 a.m. the alarm goes off. I'm awake, going goose hunting with my old hunting buddy. As I dress my dog is hyper and ready. Off we drive to our hunting place, parking and walking half a mile to our spot. Getting there, a few ducks fly over and the dog doesn't understand duck season isn't open yet. She thinks I'm too old to raise my shotgun fast enough. Then I heard honking of some high flying geese off to the side of us. I quickly raise my shotgun and give them a three-shot salute, using the excuse they were too far away for this new steel shot. In the old days using lead shot the dog would be working carrying the downed geese back to me. Oh well! A few things for sure, I heard the alarm, honking geese, flapping wings of ducks—my hearing is great. I saw the geese, ducks and morning sun—my eyes are great. I walked a half mile both ways—my legs and heart are great. And I have my friends, hunting buddy, dog and coffee click group. And I own a gun. I'm proud to be American.

That night as I sat in my easy chair with aching muscles, tired dog by my side, it proved I'm still capable of doing something, even though I've just answered my wife's question, "What have you accomplished today?" with an answer I'm now sort of regretting. My accomplishments were completed years ago. Now I'm just following President Bush's orders—go back and do your regular routine of living. As an old retired WWII and Korean vet, I follow orders given by the Commander in Chief of the United States.

As an old retired American guy, living the free life along with all Americans, I'm ready to change my routine any time to protect it again. Inside all us old guys there is no discharge date for our fight for American freedom.

Now and always it will be dated and listed as indefinite.

Class reunions, wives and cheerleaders

Although I couldn't wait for our first Webster High School Class of 1942 reunion, I never made it. From 1942-46 most of the guys and some of the girls were becoming WWII veterans. Some would be lost forever and never attend a class reunion.

The 10 year one came in 1952—I'd make that for sure. Wrong! Some of my classmates started the Webster National Guard unit after WWII. Sure enough, the call up in the Korean conflict took care of that.

1967—I'd attend the important 25th class reunion for sure. And I did. All over 40 now, most had been married for over 20 years—with some exceptions. A few were on their way to wealth and riches but most were hard working couples paying tuition for their kids going to college—of whom they were very proud, enjoying seeing them get the education they missed. Our generation's number one priority was mandated—to serve our country. None of our class of '42 had served jail time. Most were very happy, content with their families and life in general.

Of 64 graduates, 22 still lived within 50 miles of Webster. You could tell by the talk that no one thought of getting old. Some of the guys were talking about our good-looking cheerleaders, who had married our upper classmates who also served in WWII and got back before we did. It didn't seem to bother anyone too much, we all felt we married some pretty good-looking girls. We also realized married life was a whole new ball game from high school dating. Reliving old high school dreams was fun to recall, but at 42 plus we weren't up to that kind of running.

What really brought us to our senses was old Eddie Nerger—a fun guy nearing 60 who was visiting with our group. The chairman rapped his gavel and asked everyone at the banquet to return to their class tables (Eddie's class was enjoying their 40th reunion). "Eddie," we said, "You've got to sit with your class." "I'm not going to go and sit at that table with all those old people. I'm staying right here!" Everybody laughed. Eddie was young at heart, but to us he was old in age. Time goes fast.

In 1982 the class of '42 was one-third deceased—down to about 42 members. We had great attendance at our 40th reunion. We had a few millionaires now and the rest blessed with a million blessings and looking forward to early retirement. The group was showing off pictures of grandchildren and bragging how well their sons and daughters were doing. Most—with a few exceptions—were married to their first wives. Some had lost spouses and were looking. Of course talk by the guys got around to the good-looking cheerleaders we had in the class of '42. Now our wives' looks and figures equalled the cheerleaders'. Forty years makes an equalizer out of everybody. Some of the guys were getting a little baldy and potbellied also. To say nothing of graying hair. Even so, we were full of life and planning on the big one. The 50th class reunion in 1992.

The class of '42 had 90 percent attendance of the 50 percent of the class that was still alive 50 years out of high school. These old people were pushing the 70 year old mark. Now you couldn't tell the cheerleaders from the wives. Young at heart, some could still dance to the 1942 swing sounds of Glenn Miller. Of course we had our share of hip replacements and heart bypass operations to talk about. And also the great number of 50th wedding anniversaries that had been or were about to be celebrated. Even a few great-grandchildren pictures were being shown off. Because of medications and restrictions, the cash liquor bar never made a cent!

But what a great bunch of people any community would be proud to accept. They were and are "America's Greatest Generation." None were on welfare, all proud to have made it on their own. And still being an asset to their communities by doing volunteer work—not unlike other classes. But our era was not in normal times. Each decade of high school reunions will face changes like the high school classes of the 1940s.

Soon the big talk was about the 60th reunion. Just like all us guys were going to live that long and make that one.

It's now 59 years since the class of '42 graduated. Fifteen still live within 50 miles of Webster. Eight or nine of us still have coffee together almost daily. And there's talk of the 60th reunion in 2002. At least eight of us will play golf—with our bright colored golf shirts. No one could guess our age within 10 years. Laughing and joking about cheerleaders 60 years ago like it happened last night or yesterday, reliving the past, forgetting the present—these old guys pushing 80 are something else!

Supt. Frank Gellerman said in his graduation speech 60 years ago, friends you make in high school will be some of your best friends the rest of your lives. It turned out to be true.

Like all high school classes before and after, we'll leave this world in a lot better shape than we found it. But we aren't ready to go yet. We're talking about our 75th reunion already, and no doubt some of us are going to make it.

As with all reunions for the class of '42, the time comes to say good-bye to classmates, knowing as we say, God be with you, some will be with God before the next reunion—at which time they will be remembered and talked about, while those remaining laugh and joke about high school past. Including the good-looking cheerleaders and making the next reunion. Even though the odds are small, a few will make it to relive their high school days.

One thing the class of '42 did that will live forever, each and every one contributed—some more, some less—to a scholarship fund. We gave $24,000 plus to the Frank Gellerman established Centennial Fund. Each year interest from this money is given to deserving high school seniors in memory of the class of '42. As years go by we hope this endowment grows larger under sponsorship of the centennial committee. It's something other classes should look at—to preserve their class legacy. It's perpetual and lasts forever. Long after classmates cease to exist.

Have fun. Enjoy the 2001 class reunions. They go by faster than you think.

A romantic story for Valentine's Day

I feel I'm in trouble just thinking about writing this column—my Valentine story.

It was Jan. 3, 1946 and I was on a train headed home to Webster, dressed in my Class A Army uniform. It had been a hectic four weeks—the boat trip back to the states, the replacement depot, the discharge center. Now after three and a half years, most of it a combat sector overseas, here I was. Everything I owned was G.I. issue, olive drab. Even my socks and underwear. No civilian clothes, no job, wondering what lay ahead. The train seats were full of well-dressed civilians, now mostly asleep. Then came the conductor. "You'll be getting off in about 10 minutes. We'll be in Webster, we're right on tick."

It was 5 a.m., windy and cold. The only thing moving was the exhaust from George Tiegh's taxi and the dray wagon, loaded with freight. Lifting my duffel bag over my shoulder, now what! I was sure our home was locked, Dad and my two young sisters asleep. Mother had died while I was in the service. My three brothers, navy and marines were still in the service. I headed for Knapp's Cafe, where I had grown up and worked what seemed like a lifetime ago. Sure enough, the sign was on and the inside lit up. As I came in the door nothing much had changed. Even the waitress, Evelyn Flanders, just as I had remembered her. "Bobby! You're back!" she said as I put my duffel bag down and sat on the stool at the end of the counter. Right now I'll just have coffee.

In came the creamery crew, Ed Schmidt, his son Effner and Oliver Sorrell. "I bet you got a lot of war stories," and "Oh! The French gals, huh!" Yep! I was back in Webster. "What you going to do now?" they asked, when in came my old boss, Atlas Knapp. Six a.m. on the dot. "Bob, you're back," he said as he checked out the till and left for the kitchen, soon to return with a white apron in his hand. Placing it on the counter in front of me, he said, "You've been loafing for over three years. It's time you go to work. It's going to get busy in here in a little bit. You and Fran will be handling the counter."

As I looked down the counter, there appeared the prettiest, cutest girl I ever saw. Flowing hair and a figure out of this world. As she stepped in front of me she said, "Mr. Knapp wants me to show you where things are." Well now! Here I am, a chest full of combat ribbons, Sgt. stripes with two rockers and I'm going to be taking orders from her! She didn't seem one bit impressed with my medals, stripes, uniform or me. I was off to a bad start, as I took off my blouse and with my O.D. wool shirt and pants donned the white apron. It was 6 a.m., one hour after getting off the train, taking orders. No, (for my pride's sake) taking directions from the acme of all womanhood. The prettiest girl I'd ever seen. Just passing her behind the counter gave me a thrill. But everything seemed to go wrong. All the old coffee customers were coming in shaking my hand, welcoming me back. All the important businessmen—I thought that would impress her, that I was somebody. Then Atlas Knapp, the boss, right in front of her said, "Bob, you're doing more talking to the customers than serving them." Red faced now, I think I saw her smile as Atlas verbally put me down.

At 9:15 the rush was over. I asked Atlas if I could take my duffel bag home, see my dad and sisters. Atlas said, "OK, but be back by 10:15." And I was. At 2 p.m. after the dinner rush, Atlas told me, "see you at 6 a.m. tomorrow. You and Fran will handle the morning shift."

Heading to the Elevator Store, I bought new slacks, white shirts, white underwear and socks. Boy! I was going to look sharp tomorrow. Stopping back at the cafe, it was full of pretty girls waiting tables. But none impressed me as did that cold-hearted one I worked with that morning. These girls were giggly, friendly and smiled all the time when you talked to them. They told me Fran had lots of chances for dates but only went on a few. She loved to dance, didn't drink or smoke. No known steady boyfriend. I got the impression the girls liked her too.

Working at Knapp's was like old times. So was the pay. As the weeks went past I was in the bakery, kitchen, out in front. I enjoyed my old friend, Jeff Nelson, hunting rabbits, ice fishing and something else seemed to make my job enjoyable. Everyone knew. Bob was sort of chasing Fran. They had been on a few dates but Bob was a lousy dancer. But it was known around the cafe—Fran was Bob's girl.

On April 1, 1946 Atlas Knapp drew up a contract. Bob Bartos and Jeff Nelson were the new owners of Knapp's Cafe and Bakery. On April 25, while coming back from Tjelle's where I delivered bread, I stopped at the jewelry store and bought an engagement and wedding ring set. It was 11:30 a.m. as I took Fran by the hand down to our basement office, gave her the box and put the diamond ring on her finger. She sort of gasped and said, "Are you sure you really want to do this?" I knew, she knew. We wanted to. Upstairs we raced, to serve the dinner hour rush, working together at the cafe. (She often remarks, the only reason I married her was for steady cafe help.) Everyone noticed the ring. No doubt, Fran was Bob's girl.

Saturday, May 25, 1946 at 11:30 we rushed to the courthouse to get our wedding license. I didn't even have the $2 fee—I had to borrow change from Fran's apron pocket. We were getting married by the Rev. Edwin Hessel in the Methodist church after Sunday services, May 26, 1946 with only our dads and most of the cafe workers in attendance. Our honeymoon was a trip to Britton in a rented car, the banquet in a small cafe just closing for the day, an egg sandwich, a hamburger, a bottle of orange and grape pop while the waitress swept the floor. Back in Webster, to our first home, a rented apartment (the south side of the present Chuck Kuecker home on Main Street) and Monday, back to work—as a married couple.

After three great kids, we relived our marriage vows in their big weddings and banquets, six grandkids, two great-grandkids and after 55 years of working together, through the Korean War separation, hard times and good times. I still think and see Fran as I did in January, 1946. And even as I gently bump her in the kitchen of our home, I get the same thrill I did the first time behind the counter of Knapp's cafe in my G.I. uniform 55 years ago. And I think she does too, as she says "You old fool." If being content, happy, just being and wanting to be around someone you always liked is love, we have enjoyed it for 55 years.

Fishing in the old days—worth the trouble

Jeff Nelson, my partner in Knapp's Cafe and I had just seen 15 of the biggest 1 3/4-two pound perch ever caught in the late 1940s. Up to that time no one had ever seen perch that big. Not even Ury Dahling, the old-time game warden. Maybe an occasional 1 1/2 pounder, but not a mess of big ones like that. Harold Hagen, manager of the lumber yard, our fishing buddy, said a lot of guys from Grenville were catching limits like that. From three o'clock on, of all places, Waubay Lake—about a mile south of Grenville. Some muskrat trapper had found a fish line and bobber tangled in a muskrat house he was trapping. For kicks he baited the hook with a piece of muskrat meat, and in this seldom fished place he kept pulling out these jumbo perch. It took a few days before he told his buddies. Now word was out and the area was flooded with fish shacks.

Jeff, Harold and I were so excited we couldn't wait to go ice fishing. It was 1:30 p.m. Business was slow, but even with ample staff working either Jeff or I had to work. Unless we could get a good replacement manager—which left my wife, Fran. Well now, if you think she was going to get a babysitter and come to work for a dumb idea like me and Jeff going fishing, think again! When Harold said it's just too nice today, 30 degrees, those perch will be biting from 3 p.m. on, in about two hours. You guys could be back by supper rush. I knew better than that. Harold, Jeff and myself wouldn't stop fishing once we got there. Fishing will never be this good again. Just thinking I might miss out on it, which I just couldn't resist. Only thinking of myself now, and with no guts at all, I had one of the waitresses call my wife, tell her we were pretty busy and see if she would come down and help. I knew she could handle the cafe once she got there and I was sure she would handle me later, also. But right now fishing was number one.

Gathering our fishing clothes and tackle, stored in the basement of the cafe, everything was ready. Harold was waiting in the car by the lumber yard. If Fran came up the alley we would both go out the front door. If she parked in front, out the back we would go. I was stationed at the back door when I heard Jeff yell, "Here she comes." Out the back we raced.

Harold knew just where to go. It was the greatest ice fishing we ever had—jumbo perch the size of which we never knew existed. We headed home to show off our limit of trophy perch, never giving a thought to my wife working, doing my job while I'm fishing—or the trouble I might be in. In the back door of the cafe, everybody happy, talking out in front, showing off our large catch of perch, enjoying all the congratulatory comments. When I saw Fran's icy steel looks as she said, "We weren't busy at all and I'm going home now that you're here. By the way, I hope you enjoyed that fishing trip because it may cost you both. From now on I'm expensive help."

I don't know if I should blame myself, the game and fish or whom! The next two weeks the weather turned bad, blocking the lake with snow drifts. The jumbos quit biting and for the next 40 years no one ever had jumbo perch fishing again—until flood waters hit northeast South Dakota. As for my wife, it took about two days of suffering on my part, from her silent treatment—and maybe a little longer before I got kissed. Like she often said, "You're like a bent nail. No good until you're straightened out." I had it coming, but as I look back it still was the greatest ice fishing trip ever. I'm glad I didn't miss it. Fran, I think, enjoyed having me over the barrel.

But that wasn't the end. It was the game and fish guys turn to give us a little worry problem. Jeff cleaned our fish and it was our custom to place a small piece on the side of every order for our customers to taste—regardless of what they ordered. Word soon got out that Knapp's Cafe was selling local lake caught fish.

In came Ury Dahling. Our menu contained about 10 seafood items—ocean perch, northern pike, walleye, salmon, halibut steak, etc. You name it, Knapp's had it—purchased mostly from Birds Eye Frozen Foods. Ury Dahling, a tough but fair game warden started checking our freezers, inventory, checking invoices, talking to our cooks. He did this almost monthly way into spring fishing season—when a little bigger problem came up.

Jeff and I now were taking turns fishing. Eddie Majeske, Tommy Dedrickson and I went fishing in the hole off Sandy Beach at Pickerel Lake. It was midnight when we limited out. Tired, we hung a stringer of 24 walleyes in the cooler at Knapp's Cafe to show off and clean the next day. In came Ury Dahling the next morning on his monthly check. Been doing any fishing lately, he asked? Not thinking, I said, "Boy! Did I get into them last night. Limited out." Opening the cooler door there was the nicest string of 24 walleyes. "You're over limit! And over possession limit too!" He was serious. To make matters worse, Jeff showed up and said, "Ury! What do you think of the string of walleyes Bob caught?" "But they're not all mine, Eddie and Tommy were with me!" Ury again, "They have to be tagged, license number and name on them in a public locker." Me again,"This is no public locker, this is my walk-in cooler. These guys are my friends and they are coming in to pick them up."

In the back door came Tommy, saying, "What do you think of the walleyes we caught?" Ury was about to write me up, when he asked to see our fishing licenses. "Who was with you last night?" he asked Tommy. He answered, Eddie Majeske. "Well, that checks out," he said, while giving us a lecture on fish limits and storage.

Jeff took Ury up front for coffee. Our problem was solved, no ticket, no write up. Ury was mumbling about how tough all the new GF&P regulations were getting (and this was 50 years ago).

Thinking back about how guilty I felt fishing when I should have been working in the olden days—and how much fun it was. It now seems dull fishing when I really have all the time and my wife even encourages such trips just to get me out of her way. It's no longer the thrill it used to be. It was a big thrill to show off the big fish when I should have been working. everyone was impressed and said great things about the catch. Now-a-days if I catch a big fish someone always comments, "Sure he should catch big fish. That's all he's got to do."

One thing for sure, my thrill of fishing might have diminished, but the thrill I get from tricks I play on Fran is still the same as over 50 years ago. Maybe more so.

The signs of spring— how they change

Oh! How times have changed—even the first signs of spring from 1930 to 2001. Today, for me spring means hearing the first robin sing. I can't wait for the golf course to open or try out that new fishing reel I got for Christmas. Or shooting my Benelli shotgun during spring snow goose hunt, which will probably miss us because of all the snow cover. How lucky us old guys are to be living the good life in the spring of 2001. And we sort of smile as we hear the young guys say, "What are those old dudes on anyway! How do they dream up all that old time stuff? I can't imagine anything like that ever happening!" (Yet most of them add to it and all the old guys swear it's true—just listen to them.)

The first sign of spring back in the 1930s was mean old clucking hens when we went to pick eggs. You had to throw them off the nest to keep from getting your hands pecked. We didn't have time to listen to robins sing. Then there was the chicken coop to clean and haul out. Which wasn't as bad as the Webster city crew who had to shovel piles of horse manure in the back alley (back of Knapp's Cafe) where the bobsled teams were tied every day during winter while farmers were shopping.

Then there were housecleaning chores. I don't care how good a housekeeper a woman was, everyone had a bedbug problem. Outside with the mattress and taking apart the bed. Outside with the bedsprings, pouring kerosene all over the steel springs, killing the bedbugs and their eggs. Dusting the mattress with a yellow powder after beating it with a rug beater. Haven't heard of bedbugs in the last 50 years, but in the 30s every household had some.

Flights of geese honking most every spring night, circling the lighted Main Street, which they thought was water—because in the 1930s sloughs were dry. That was a sign of spring.

Carrying out rotten potatoes, squash and pumpkins from the cellar—the leftover supply of winter inventory—by the pail and tub full. What a rotten, stinking mess that was. Another sign of spring from the cellar in the 30s.

Webster businessmen, every day sweeping the sidewalk in front of their stores, even washing sidewalks down with a hose. Washing the windows. And a sure sign of spring was when city drinking fountains—with a step on them so little kids could reach the top—were turned on. I remember three—one on each corner of the block starting at the drug store, Klein Hotel corner and on the corner of the present day Flower Cart building. Also a sure sign of spring was the horse watering trough across the street from the lumber yard being filled. It still exists today and is used at the livestock section of the fairgrounds.

The 1930s produced spring fun times too. Like the spring trip to Grenville—to a creek where men were spearing suckers with pitchforks. Dad would always get a gunnysack of fish for a bottle of his homemade chokecherry wine. Oh, yes! There were always a few illegal northerns in the sack also. Dad would scale the northerns with a butcher knife and mother would bake the big northerns. I don't ever remember seeing a filet knife in the 30s. Nobody filleted fish. It was considered a waste of meat. Everyone who ate fish picked out the bones after the fish was cooked. Carp and suckers were smoked, salted and eaten cold. This was a three-day process. Also, Mother would pickle northerns in fruit jars. Another sign of spring in the 30s.

Being the first kids at the city dump to pick up bottles and wash them out, we could sell pop bottles for a penny, beer bottles for three cents. A discarded copper boiler or worn out aluminum tea kettle were valuable finds which would bring 12 cents at Rohde's junkyard. Aluminum was cheaper. We would make enough money for the 10 cent matinee at Lyric Theater and if we got there early Charlie Bailey would give us half a sack of grannies out of the popcorn machine free!

Going along the railroad tracks and tree groves looking for asparagus sprouts was fun. As was setting our traps for pocket gophers and snaring striped gophers for bounty payments of two cents a tail. Every kid had a stinking Prince Albert can full of them and another with pocket gopher claws and tails, 10 cent bounty.

All memories of spring in the 30s. But this is the spring of 2001 and if my golf game doesn't improve this year, I'm going to get a dozen traps and try some of that 1930 pocket gopher trapping. That's one thing that hasn't changed in the last 70 years. Except a 39 cent trap now costs $8.79. But the art of trapping remains the same. Asparagus sprouts still can be found in the trees. Gone are town chicken coops, horse manure piles, drinking water fountains, dump pile raids and the city horse trough has lost its city location. And one sure thing—the bedbugs are gone forever. But the creek by Grenville still produces a spring run of carp and suckers, and I'm sure a few northern pike get eaten too. But not like in the 1930s. Today northern are filleted and most of the bones removed for easier eating. No scaling with a butcher knife. Now it's an electric filleting knife—removes most of the bones, wastes a lot of meat.

I'll let the young guys of today talk about the spring of 2002 in 2078—and let them explain to the young guys of 2078 how they remember it. I'm sure the old guys of 2078 will get the same reaction as my dad got telling of springs in the 1890s and I got in 2001 telling of the 1930s. I'm sure glad life and progress get better each spring. I hated those bedbugs, clucking hens and cleaning chicken coops.

The Mysterious Man in the coon-skin coat

Since writing the story about Awalt Becker's livery barn, I thought it might prove interesting to write about the man. Awalt Becker—a Webster Main Street character for over 50 years.

He was sort of the center of gravity for everyone's eyes as he navigated from tavern to tavern in his heavy coonskin coat and muskrat fur cap, using a diamond carved willow cane. He walked erect, much like a full army colonel who had just been promoted to general coming from his promotional party.

Under this coonskin coat he wore a fine, but old wool Pendleton shirt, tie with a gold nugget stickpin, wool suit coat and pants. His shoes were high top kid leather, years old and scuffed up—much like his old dirty grease stained wrinkled suit, shirt and tie.

The man inside this outside apparel was very gentlemanly. He never ate a meal and seemed to live off beer. Always erect, he was never bow shouldered or in the gutter in public. Maybe a little stiff legged and wobbly, but he never staggered or fell, even in old age.

He was never noticed much in the summer, but spring, fall and winter the man in the long coonskin fur coat, muskrat fur cap and diamond willow cane was a Main Street attraction.

I think old Mink Bedessem the barber explained Awalt Becker best. A real gentleman of high rank and peculiar odor.

I knew of Awalt Becker for over 50 years. I heard all the hearsay and rumors about him. Some were justified, some not. From my early childhood I saw Awalt Becker around the livery barn that us kids played in. I remember him mostly in flared hunting pants, high laced boots, hunting coat and cap, guiding out-of-state hunters pheasant and duck hunting, riding in their big, high powered cars. At night these hunters were dressed in fancy suits, wearing big, wide-brimmed felt hats, ordering expensive steaks, illegally pouring liquor from fancy silver flasks and leaving the waitress mega tips. But they appeared to be perfect gentlemen, talking among themselves, sort of ignoring everyone else. Of course everyone said they had to be big city gangsters. Just like the rumor that Awalt Becker had been a bootlegger. But that era was long past. Where else did he get his money he spent in the bars all the time? Awalt always acted like a man of means.

How did he acquire a half-section of land east of Webster, 80 acres and a hunting lodge in Clark County, the livery barn? He never had a job, never farmed. The land was mostly slough and rock, the 80 acres in Clark County was mostly water, the building seldom used. In later years it was lost to taxes. How he managed to always have money or where he got it from to pay taxes was a mystery.

I never saw Awalt eat a meal or drink coffee and I was on Main Street most of his life. He never had a job, never farmed, yet was never a burden to anyone. He rented out his farm buildings for less than the yearly taxes. He kept 20 acres with a shack to sleep in at night, moving into an apartment in Dustrud's apartment house in the last years of his life.

He appeared to me to be well educated, by the soft manner of speech and polite manners. He always appeared healthy, but while taking a high school class tour of Peabody Hospital, Art Lundquist showed us an alcohol jar containing a 36 inch tape worm. The caption label read, "Taken from Awalt Becker." Although I can't remember a day of him ever being sick, for a guy who drank so much beer and never ate meals, it's said he had stomach problems. But I never knew of a day he missed making rounds of the local taverns.

For a man everyone saw on Main Street almost daily, no one, to my knowledge, really knew Awalt Becker, a bachelor with no known family. All the time I knew him, his only background was reputation given him by local people, built on hearsay and pure rumor. A man who always paid his own way with a bad beer drinking habit.

Awalt Becker remains a mystery to me and most everyone else on Main Street.

He must have loved animals—and most of the Main Street dogs followed that coonskin coat. If Awalt stopped to talk to a friend, dogs were always marking it. More than one person remarked about this happening almost daily. Yet warm, shine, cold, blizzard or snow, Awalt wore that coonskin coat.

To us old timers it doesn't seem that long ago that Awalt Becker left Main Street in his coonskin fur coat. His death was about as mysterious as his life. It was rumored that he died of food poisoning because some half-eaten moldy weiners were found in his dresser drawer in the Dustrud rooming house.

I remember helping pack his personal belongings after his death. The 30 pound stinking coonskin coat, muskrat hat and diamond willow cane and shipping them to some distant cousin who claimed them. All that remains of Awalt Becker is hearsay and rumored reputation. But to local people, the man wearing the coonskin coat, muskrat cap and diamond willow cane will remain in our memories until we cease to exist. It proves, once again, it takes all kinds to make a Main Street. Whether Awalt Becker added to or detracted from Main Street, the reader can decide.

Livery barns—different styles, same smell

From the 1920s-30s the home place was 511 West First Street, in the middle of the block across the street from Lumber Store-N-More. One block from Main Street and one block from the railroad tracks. I grew up between two giant horse manure piles. Less than 50 feet from our back door to the south, contributed to by Henry Duryee's two barns and Awalt Becker's huge livery barn made the pile 150 feet to the north.

Duryee, a rural mail carrier owned two livery barns. One had cow and horse stalls for Lewis Bicknell's horse (Major) and the other cash rented by the day or night to farmers who drove teams, wagons and buggies to town for supplies. County roads were mostly dirt trails and winter was mostly bobsled travel. In the '20s-'30s furnishing feed, water and shelter for horses was a good business.

Duryee was a righteous man—no cussing or tom foolery around his place. He catered to well-to-do farmers with expensive teams and rigs. The barns were surrounded by a seven-foot wood fence with an extended roof to shelter wagons and buggies. Also stored in this area were two old stagecoaches—one with Wells Fargo written on it—an old horse drawn hearse, a couple of enclosed US Mail wagons on bobsled runners and, of course, a huge manure pile outside this compound facing our house.

As kids we pretty much left Duryee's barns alone. But we couldn't resist digging a hole under the wooden fence and playing cowboy and Indian on the stagecoach—bouncing on the spring drivers seat. We got caught once playing in the haymow, because we scared a setting hen who did so much squawking it attracted Mrs. Duryee's attention. She had us come in the house and gave us cookies, all the time lecturing us on how we could get hurt and playing in the barn was not proper. Whether it was how nice she treated us or plain respect for Duryee's barn, we sort of ignored their property. But their manure pile stunk just as bad as the one to the north of our house.

Becker's livery barn was a fun place. It was one of the biggest structures in Webster—20 two-horse stalls on the main level with a big bay window in the front office, a big haymow with a partitioned off front area with bunk rooms and living quarters. As five, six and seven year olds we knew that barn. We knew every escape route in and out when somebody yelled at us to get out of there! But it was more fun to sit and be quiet up in the haymow, listening to the giggling and laughing of grown ups on the other side of that partitioned off area.

It was prohibition. No booze was legal, but we knew something fun was going on. Last week, reading a Reporter & Farmer from June 6, 1927: Atty. Harris secures order against local women—liquor found by officers in raid—restraining order has been granted against three employees from the building owned by Caroline Becker for the purpose of drinking intoxicating liquor or any other immoral purpose or action. That reference brought back all my childhood memories. On with my story.

Becker's barn had mostly younger farmers with old rigs and high spirited horses. The men treated us kids—sometimes with pennies and nickels, even half a sack of candy. Even the wobbly guys who came from upstairs were nice to us. Unlike the old guys at Duryee's, who pushed us aside.

We kids learned a lot about life in this three barn half block area. Like when Duryee's cow, Goldie was about to give birth to a calf. Mrs. Duryee came to the barn and sent all us boys home, saying "this is nothing for you boys to see." After waiting all afternoon we were going to miss the main event, being told we could see the calf the next day.

After a couple of weeks a mare was brought to Becker's barn. Doc Chapman told us she would be delivering a colt in about half an hour. "Be quiet and don't disturb her," he said. We asked if we could watch, remembering the Duryee calf deal. "Just stay out of the way and be quiet," Doc said. We would, and we did.

This time we saw, in disbelief, the colt arrive. We watched as it struggled, staggered and wobbled to its feet, acting much like some of the guys we watched coming down from upstairs. Doc said "He'll be OK as soon as he starts nursing. He's hungry now." We knew what that meant because we had watched the two-week old calf do that. But that's all we knew until then!

We liked Doc Chapman better than Mrs. Duryee. We got to see the main event this time! It was so quiet in the barn—all the horses were just as motionless, wide-eyed as us kids.

Back to the manure piles. In the fall everyone in our whole neighborhood would put tar paper around the bottom of their homes and bank it with horse manure to insulate it and conserve energy. In the spring it was spread on the garden and plowed under for fertilizer. Us kids said we wouldn't eat anything from that garden. However, as strawberries ripened, carrots and peas we forgot the stinking horse manure. We all ate more than our share, raw from the garden.

Henry Duryee's house still exists today, south of our old home place. One of the barns that surrounded it was moved to the country, one still stands on the present day Norm Knispel place south city limits—the place Henry Duryee bought and retired to.

Becker's livery stable and barn had many owners. Later known as Wang's Garage, it was torn down and replaced by the present day VFW building.

One thing in closing. As a six year old I didn't understand what was going on or what all the giggling and laughing was about in that partitioned off area in Becker's haymow. At 79 years old I had to read it in an old Reporter & Farmer just to find out. So read the paper if you want to know for sure what's going on!

Complaints take their toll at coffee

Just maybe it's that I was too busy in years past making a living that I didn't notice the weather, but the winter of 2001 was the worst in my memory. Windy, cold, spring raining, damp, maybe two hours of sunshine in a week. And it was taking a toll on the old guys' coffee click at the diner. Talk was going from good times in the past to bitching about the present.

First there was Shorty, saying "I've went by Shorty for over 60 years. That's my name. Everybody knows me by that name. My best friend is Dizzy Burns. I doubt if anyone knows his real name. Then there's Slim, Skinny, Baldy and a lot of others. I think nicknames are sort of an honor. Like in England, they give out nicknames as an honor from the queen. Like Sir, Lord, Count. Now some jerk is saying nicknames are politically incorrect. What those incorrect political rascals need to do is start working for a living instead of getting a free ride. Starting trouble about something they know nothing about. I know I don't take offense to being called Shorty. And neither does Baldy, Slim or Dizzy. It's been that way for 60 years!

"Then there's those do-rights who want to change the name of athletic teams from Braves and Arrows because it hurts their feelings. I knew and grew up with a lot of Indian dads and they thought just like I do."

Hey, hey! Shorty, let's get off this subject because all us old guys are starting to agree with you. But no one was stopping Shorty this morning. "OK," he said. " I like the smell of burning leaves and bonfires burning trash. And it was a lot cheaper than bagging. You can't do that anymore in town either. I remember when behind every store in Webster in the alley was a big trash burner, burning boxes and paper. Nerger's, Elevator

Store, Woodwards, Halbkat's Drug. Everybody had one. Tjelle even had a smoke house in the alley to smoke hams, sausage and wieners. In fact Knapp's Cafe, Red Owl Store and Elevator Store had fires going all the time, right in the alley next to the lumber yard. And no businesses burned down because of them, either."

Well, Shorty. The asphalt stopped burning in the alleys and streets. That's why.

Shorty again, "I think it was all those second-hand smoke people. And this is a democracy. If 51 percent of the people like to smell smoke, then we have that right. Today a couple of people with a news media's outlet can make 98 percent of the rest of the people suffer with their radical views."

There's no stopping Shorty this morning. Maybe we can sway the talk to women. Shorty always has a comment or two on that subject. Like women's hairdos. "Remember when your mother would get a finger wave? Or a marcell? I'll bet if your wife would go into a beauty shop and say 'Give me a finger wave or a marcell,' nobody would know what she was talking about. They wear their hair nowadays looking like they came out of a windstorm."

Here we go again! Shorty was unstoppable. "And the shoes they wear! I liked high heels. Now they wear old clodhoppers that look like they came out of a farm field for dress. China made tennis shoes. Where are the ladies of yesterday! All I see in the summer is belly buttons and shorts."

Oh, shut up, Shorty! Yesterday is gone. Wake up—we're in 2001. I like the way the young girls look. They have and are their own person. Back in our day the girls I knew were bashful. It was hard to get a yes or no. Nowadays talk to any young person—they look you straight in the eye and tell you right off what they think. Whether you agree or not. Frank and honest. And they don't have to be 75 years old either, like us, to be knowledgeable. The world is changing, so are the people who live in it.

Well, it's about time for a coffee refill and this morning's coffee click had been nothing but bitching, preaching and Shorty! And I was hoping something would come up that was interesting. Something usually does.

Right now I don't know if it's that second cup of coffee, Shorty or the rotten spring weather. I've got a burning stomach and when I get home I'm going to have to start doing yard work.

While paying for coffee, an old gal came up and said, "I read your story on Lawrence Welk, and I think he was a great dancer. How would you know he wasn't? Did you ever dance with him? Well I did!" Now that really made my day. At least one person read my column!

Up to their knees in feathers

I wanted to write a column about Wist Produce Co., one of Webster's biggest and oldest business employers, but in my research I couldn't find who founded the business or the date it started. I know it existed long before 1928.

The first boss of the operation, and I believe owner was Lawrence B. Wist. It was located one block west of Webster power plant for over 65 years of my lifetime—until it ceased operation and was torn down.

Wist Produce Co. was a big wooden structure next to the railroad tracks with about 25 full-time employees and 50-60 temporary people always on call. Webster's first ice cream store—with 20 flavors—was added onto the north side of the office. In fact I don't remember a time between 1930 to the early '50s that some addition or remodeling wasn't being done.

From 1925 or maybe earlier, to 1950 I would be safe in saying every farmer in Day County did business with Wist Produce. Selling furs, cow hides, eggs, chickens, turkeys, geese and ducks.

Nellie Swant, a friend of my mother (who also acted as a midwife in the area) was a full-time foreman of the egg candling department, which was a full-time operation with 8-10 women. A 30-dozen case of eggs would be graded at a time. I remember watching as Nellie would open that top of the case, take out the divider and grab three eggs in each hand. She put them up to a small box with a quarter-sized hole with a light bulb behind it and sort of x-rayed the eggs, one at a time. Also there was a scale where she would weigh each egg. This was called grading. Most women grading eggs could do only two at a time in each hand. Nellie was a loud-talking boss. Nobody interfered with her department and if someone did, her actions would make an Army drill sergeant blush! I doubt if a larger refrigerated and freezing plant existed anywhere than Wist Produce had. Boxcars were filled daily for shipment both east and west.

Chickens by the thousand, by the truckload were hauled to Wist Produce. In the basement was a chain conveyor belt with chicken feathers steaming wet; school kids, women and men in knee-high rubber boots stripped feathers off chickens for five cents each, standing in wet feathers knee deep. These birds were then packed 12 to a box and put in the freezer to be shipped out. I can't remember, but believe the chickens were not cleaned inside, but frozen whole.

Turkeys, ducks and geese were plucked and packed the same way, to be shipped out in refrigerated box cars. You might have to be 65 or older to remember that, but few people I know in the Webster area didn't at one time work or sell at Wist Produce. Even eggs the stores bought ended up at Wist's.

Carloads of cowhides, rabbits frozen by the boxcar load, the railroad siding by Wist Produce always had five or six cars being loaded. It's my belief that Armour and Co. owned or backed the operations from 1933 on. Peter Monzel and L.B. Wist started Monzel Beer Distributing Company in 1935—both were Armour employees at that date—of Wist Produce Co.

I'll never forget the tame duck and goose pond across the tracks where they were kept— and the wild ducks and geese the pond attracted in the fall. It was a mad scramble catching and sacking them when it came time for processing them. Also, feeding time was something to see. As close to the tracks as the pond was located, I don't recall loud trains passing by affecting them.

A lot of Webster people got their first jobs working for L.B. Wist and a few spent their life working there.

L.B. Wist established an egg cracking operation at Wist Produce in the war years. They separated yolks from whites, placed them in 10-gallon 30-pound tins or buckets with lids, froze and shipped them out by the carload under contract by the US government. As liability laws and sanitary regulations became more effective Wist Produce's operation became more ineffective. L.B. Wist also owned Wist Lockers on Main Street, with an ice cream parlor in the front of the store (where Mahlen's insurance is located now).

L.B. Wist retired in 1958 after over 30 years in business, selling his holding in Peter Monzel Co., locker plant and ice cream operation.

In the mid '30s Wist built the home Lonnie Vander Linden now owns. He had two sons, Robert, a naval cadet flying officer who died in WWII flight training and Burton, who visits Webster and lives in Arizona.

L.B. Wist served Webster in many civic positions, always in a white shirt and tie. His employees considered him a great boss, a friendly person who got along with everybody, fair and just. An outstanding Webster area booster, he managed and owned an operation that did an outstanding job of making and building the Webster area with a service the town and county needed to develop into a lasting community.

Other operators after Wist could not keep up with the changing times and Wist Produce closed its doors some 20 years ago. Just another industry built in Webster to create the town of Webster, now only a part of Webster's founding history.

Crisis in Roslyn, Grenville— no Copenhagen

Everyone is fed up with the 2001 weather—snow piled up six or seven feet high on every boulevard in Day County. Writing and talking about it even makes it seem worse. One thing for sure, the only job in the world you can be 80-100 percent wrong on and still get paid is weather forecasting. Like that good-looking silver tongued TV weather guy, "The storm will go south of your area. Northeast South Dakota will get only a trace of snow." Well those mild flurries with only a trace of snow amounts to five inches and drifts three-feet high. And a blocked driveway, some of which is caused by the city snowplow. I don't know if those expensive Doppler radar systems caused the problem that the TV guy keeps referring to or if old man weather left his post and let the kid run things, but one thing for sure, the wrong lever got pulled on northeast South Dakota.

South Dakota is the land of infinite variety and nobody is ever going to guess the weather in northeast South Dakota 100 percent. I don't care how many years of weather college you attend, any northeast South Dakota farmer will tell you farming and weather are a gamble. Predicting and guessing are part of the game. As for being paid for it, that's questionable. A lot of farmers don't get paid when planting too early or late, but the TV weather guy does, right or wrong. If I'm going to take my snow blowing frustration out on somebody it might as well be the TV weatherman.

Long before the TV weather guy, some 65 years ago, Roslyn and Grenville had a snowbound crisis caused by weeks of snowstorms. Roads were blocked, water pumps frozen. Water was being bucketed from wells. But those people were well prepared. A Norwegian or Polish wife could make a great meal if she had flour or sugar and this was running out. Staple items in their stores were depleted. What was even worse was the men were three or four days out of their main staple of life—Copenhagen snuff.

It was almost like a town meeting when about 20 of the best teams and bobsleds and three neighbors to each sled decided to make the 12-mile trip through blocked roads and drifts to Webster to resupply their families. The trip meant shoveling with heavy scoop shovels (not the light aluminum kind we have today) through a half-mile of drifts they couldn't avoid. Six miles north of Webster, by the tree claim going to Grenville, they were joined by the Grenville crew. They arrived in Webster about 3 p.m. It was like a big parade. Webster people were cheering them that winter day.

(Some seven years later, when feeling homesick stationed at an England air base, I would recall those bobsleds and the men with shovels held high as our B-17 returned from a bombing run and the flight crews were cheered by the base support group guys for a successful bombing mission accomplished. It was one way to take a guy's mind off of hardship, remembering the old South Dakota days instead of the war.)

After unhitching the horses they were watered, fed and sheltered in three delivery barns, two located on Henry Duerre's place west across the street from UBC on the corner of Fifth Avenue and First Street. Both barns are now gone, the house remains as it was. Henry Duerre, a retired mail carrier bought the present day Norm Knispel farm on Hwy. 25, selling the house to Herb Peterson, the oilman who owned what is now Thompson Oil Co., across the street from the house. Mr. Duerre then moved one of the barns to the Norm Knispel farm where it stands today. Ewalt Becker's livery barn, where the present day VFW Club is located was also used, but it was torn down years ago.

Webster businessmen had arranged a free meal for the 50-60 bobsled men from Roslyn and Grenville. Ed Nerger, Alfred Hagen from the Elevator Store and old man Tjelle were taking grocery lists and orders and passing out free boxes of Copenhagen to everyone. Atlas Knapp had a cigar by every plate. Even the medicine men, Frank Halbkat and Floyd Cornwell were there taking prescription orders. They also sold liquor and I'm sure there were some orders for that also being taken and packaged. I remember carrying dishes and coffee through all the people in a packed cafe. Most of the bobsled crew was planning on staying the night, sleeping in the clean straw in the barns, using horsehide robes and blankets. Free beer was being served at Bailey Pool Hall. The bobsledders were Webster's guests and the businessmen their hosts.

Six a.m. the next morning, breakfast and to the stores, packing boxes of groceries in the bobsleds, a couple filled with coal. The wind was in the south, everyone was happy, heading for the 12-mile trip home.

It was said there was a trail of brown tobacco spit all the way to Roslyn from Webster that day.

It was a wintery day I'll never forget and I pride my column on not writing fiction. I'm sure there are some old guys or wives that remember that bobsled trip from Roslyn and the Grenville area, or heard about it. The first two to call and tell me (605) 345-3779, I'll give a free Memories of the Millennium book. I know it really happened, but I would like a little reader proof.

A morning in my coffee click

My story assignment was history of Peabody Hospital. After a lot of boring research, I said the heck with it and went for coffee.

Webster has been known as a town of clicks—small social groups that associate together, usually by age, business, church groups, retired or just plain mixed up coffee groups. Which is not all bad.

My coffee group consists of 75-year-old guys and older. Then there is the business group, the 50-year group. They are still paying their civic rent—serving on boards, city council, church activities and the like. Sort of the movers and shakers of the town and business community. There is also the retired women's group. The men call this the gossip's group, but they really have a lot of laughter coming from their table. Notice I didn't mention the age of this click—which is varied and mostly very mature.

Well, the topic this morning in my group was mostly how long we were going to live. One guy in the group had just read George Burns' book, How to Live to be 100 or More. The ultimate diet, sex and exercise book. Science and health care are moving so fast these days. Well now! They were moving pretty fast a long time ago. Remember George washington? He had wooden teeth. Yeah! His wife Martha had a lot of splinters taken out of her lips—that was one of the side effects. That's an old joke, too. Another guy, "Well, they have come a long way. They can replace a hand with an artificial one." So what? Back in the pirate days they replaced a hand with a steel hook. Yeah! Again the joker speaks, "But every time he scratched himself he couldn't sit down for a week. And the same was true with the pirate with the wooden leg if he kicked you." The laughter at our table was louder than the women's today.

Some of the guys at the table had a steel knee replacement, one a steel hip socket and in came another to join us with a steel knee replacement using a walker. One of the healthier guys said, "All you guys got to worry about with all this artificial steel replacements is a safe place to go when thunder and lightning hits the area. Or rusting out. You guys don't need a doctor. You need a good mechanic, lube job and 1,000 mile checkup instead of a physical. You guys won't be dying anymore, and if you do blow a gasket you can leave your bodies to the junk yard instead of a medical university."

They have replacement parts for everything. Pretty soon they will have places where you can pick out a kidney, liver, heart—they already have eye banks. It's not as far fetched as it sounds. A good reliable replacement place might even give you a free 10-day trial, and if it doesn't work out you can return it. The joker speaks again, "There's one item I'd like to try out for 10 days." Another guy, "A face lift, you mean, don't you?" A roar of laughter was drawing more people to our table. I was having a good time laughing with my old buddies, and I've forgotten my deadline for the Peabody Hospital story due today.

Most at the table were worrying about their insides, but their outsides needed a lot of work too. Some guy said, "No longer tall, dark or handsome, now shriveled, dumpy and pale. Even potbellied." Well now, we are young at heart. Let's see. Maybe we could take a lesson from that good-looking women's group at the table back there. Or the movie queens like Joan Collins and Debbie Reynolds who are 65-plus and look like 36. All we need is a face lift, a wig, a little exercise to take off the potbelly, and we could all be looking 40 years younger. Because we are all young at heart.

I don't know. I'm pretty content with things just the way they are. And I don't think our wives would put up with all the time we would have to spend in the bathroom getting ready to go for coffee. Half the time I don't even comb my hair—just put on my cap and come down here to have coffee and talk and laugh with you guys. It makes the time go faster and by the sounds of the talk this morning we got a lot of time left. And a lot of replacements for our worn out parts too—if we don't run into a steel shortage. Life is great. I'm going to relax and enjoy my next 20 years 'til I'm 100. Besides, I might end up changing so many parts I could end up being a boring historian. I'd hate that.

I'm sorry if I bored my readers with my coffee hour talk, but I enjoyed writing it—even if I left out some parts that would make the associate editor's face red.

I also want to wish all the readers of the Reporter & Farmer a very happy new year and thanks for the many letters you have sent us. It makes me feel very humble and appreciative of your acknowledgement of my column. Also, thanks for ordering my book. Also, the local people who make me feel good by remarking they read my column. I sincerely appreciate it.

31

Multi-million dollar company started here

I wonder how many readers of this column realize as they pay their monthly electric bill to NorthWestern Public Service that the company originated here in Webster. And that includes about 15 towns to the south, west and north of Webster, established back in the 1920s by Mid-West Electric Co., which would form the nucleus of NWPS, the multi-million dollar corporation we know today.

In 1910-1920 Webster was a growing city, as were the towns in all of South Dakota. Webster, a city of 2,000 people, gravel streets, wood sidewalks, horse and buggies, wooden buildings. Gas and kerosene lamps were being replaced by electric lights, some gas motors were being replaced with electric, there were washing machines, electric vacuum cleaners, salesmen were selling electric wiring and lights, even some iceboxes were being switched to refrigerators with no thought of where the power was coming from—or wiring to get it there.

Webster had bought a gas generator to supply electricity to the street lights and city. Webster had at least three forming electric companies. Everyone was selling electric items, everybody was stringing wire—over rooftops, around chimneys, in trees, on fences. everything was makeshift and temporary. This ad, run by Webster Electric Co. is quoted from the Dec. 22, 1910 Reporter & Farmer: "If you can't afford to wire the whole house or rent one, why not? Have one or two lights installed in your living rooms in such a way that you could take the lamp and wiring with you when you move."

By July 8, 1920 Webster was a tangled mess of wires. No code, no directions, really not an electrician in town—just people making money selling wire and light bulbs. Some days they had power, some days not, and nights—none.

Again I quote from the Reporter & Farmer. Webster commercial club drafted a resolution to the city council: "Under the present operation of the city electric power plant no current is furnished for lighting or power purposes or fuel during evening hours, holidays or Sundays. As a county seat town electric power should be provided seven days a week, both nights and days."

In 1921 Clarence J. Strike, whose dad owned and operated an electrical distribution plant and company in New Hampton, IA and his friend, Everett A. Sewell came to Webster. They were later joined by Sam Strike and Cornelius Wells. Everett and Clarence recognized Webster's electrical nightmare and headaches. A tangled mess of wiring with no code, no direction, lack of power source. After getting city council's approval to take over operation of the city power plant they set up a new electric company, Mid-West Electric. They started to restructure the fly-by-night companies. With the help of Sam Strike and Corny Wells training linemen and electricians, E.A. Sewell and C.J. Strike started merging companies and buying out some—not only in Webster but in all the towns southwest and northwest of Webster. Including watertown's early power plant. E.A. Sewell would later handle the sale of the power building back to the city of Watertown. C.J. Strike would take wiring crews as far as Timber Lake to wire schools. There is a legendary story of Sam Strike driving a Model A Ford across the Missouri River railroad bridge on ties when the ferry was broken down, to get to Timber Lake.

Again from the Reporter & Farmer, "Mid-West Electric will be displaying and installing equipment of their own development and design in the new Webster School—inter-communications telephone signaling equipment, fire alarms, classroom electric clocks with a master clock, call bells, electric control heating." A wiring contract way beyond its time in the state, companies and visitors from in-state and out came just to see and copy their original developments.

Sewell and Strike, with Mid-West Electric managed to build and service not only Webster, but 15 other towns with great service and rates. And it was being noticed by many people hundreds of miles away. Webster people just took great enterprises like Peabody Hospital and Mid-West Electric for granted—thinking it was developed here, it will stay here. Not so! On April 7, 1927 some corporate thinkers decided to acquire Mid-West Electric and its founders, E.A. Sewell and C.J. Strike, merging them with a new company called Northwestern Public Service. E.A. Sewell, reluctant to relocate, became executive officer of the

Webster area of towns. C.J. Strike would leave Webster for Huron, to oversee the new operation and become Northwestern Public Service's new president. Everett died in 1981, Clarence long before that. Sam Strike and Cornelius Wells have also passed away.

Everett A. Sewell lived in Webster for over 60 years. He had two sons, Warren, who after serving in the Korean War returned to serve Webster in dentistry for over 40 years; now retired, he is my coffee buddy and Steve, who sort of followed his dad's footsteps and was a senior vice president of Northwestern Public Service. Retiring in Webster, he passed away only a couple of years ago. We should be proud to recognize Webster people's accomplishments and the assets they are in making Webster a great town.

Somehow it still irks me that an early lack of leadership on the part of the city of Webster let a multi-million dollar corporation like north-western Public Service, which originated here, slip away. The line crews, appliance store and billing office operation have almost ceased to exist here, as well as the many good paying jobs.

Make no mistake about the foundation Mid-West Electric built in the 1920s in towns they serviced. With few exceptions they are being served by the same company they merged with 80-some years ago, including Webster.

The next time you're paying your electric bill to NorthWestern, just remember—that company is also part of Webster's past history.

32

What happened to Day County's bakeries

What happened to all the bakeries that operated in Day County? One in Bristol, Town's Bakery in Waubay and Webster had two, Ballard Hicks' Cowboy Bread and Knapp's Cafe and Bakery—Butter Crust. All had great histories, but I'm going to play favorites because I grew up in Knapp's and I know the history of how it ran and what caused the downfall of so many of South Dakota's bakeries. After years of service to communities in Day County, in less than six months during the years of 1938-40, what could have stopped a booming business?

I watched the development of Knapp's Bakery and Cafe from a coal fired cake oven to the first oil fired rotary oven to the first bread slicing machine, automatic bread mixer, automatic donut maker—always ahead of his time. He furnished a variety of pastry and bread products all over northeast South Dakota. A standing order of 100-150 loaves of bread was put on the train at 5 a.m. three days a week for stores in Aberdeen and daily truck routes handled towns of Butler, Lily, Crocker, Bradley, Crandall, Roslyn, Grenville and the lakes.

Outstanding bakers from Chicago and Minneapolis—Joe Sparrow, Fred McFadden trained local employees in the art of Danish pastries. French doughnuts, always first in the area in tens of different varieties of breads, cookies, rolls. The first to offer two breads baked in one loaf—half white, half wheat. And oh! The fruit cakes made with real rum shipped out all over the USA.

There never has been, nor will it ever exist again, the homemade from scratch variety of daily made bakery products whose recipes existed only in the minds of those great master bakers. Profit margins were figured in pennies. Service and quality products made the bakery.

Atlas Knapp, creator of Knapp's Bakery and Cafe had an outstanding business brain as owner-operator-community leader. He was Webster's first fire chief, served as mayor, on school board and many other ways.

No church ever paid for a bakery order—it was his donation. He demanded the best from his 36-40 employees—he was around overseeing all the time. A baker caught drinking rum meant for the fruit cake was fired on the spot—as was a waitress who was five minutes late the second time. You were expected to be five minutes early, uniform neat and pressed.

At six years old, 1928, I was hanging around the kitchen, where my mother was one of the cooks. Atlas came in, "No loafing in here!" I was told to scrape dishes for the dish washers. By the age of 10 I was working in the bakery. By 12 I was chief bread delivery man to all five grocery stores, getting my first paycheck ($1.50) and free meals. In 1934 my work schedule was 4:30-9 a.m., then school, noon hour clean tables, 4-8 p.m. clean the bakery. Saturday and Sunday were 12-hour days. Atlas Knapp was a school board member and expected me to keep above average grades in school also, because it was a reflection on him if I failed to do so. And he was really teaching me a trade, which I should consider worth something. Believe it or not, I enjoyed my life. I had a job.

Businessmen and people from all over the state came to look at Knapp's Cafe and Bakery's first line of equipment. The first Carrier commercial air conditioned cafe, first terrazzo marble floor, fireproof wall paneling, first soda and ice cream counter, first steam table for keeping food hot, first electric national cash register, first automatic dishwasher, automatic potato peeler, deep fat fryer, shoestring potato cutter, butter chip maker, milk dispenser cooler, first cigarette machine, penny peanut machine. I can't remember them all—each a marvel of its time. Even at Atlas Knapp's house, which still stands today at 427 W. 10th Ave., has the first red tile roof in Webster. This is not a first of Knapp's Bakery, but the first hot shower other than a tub bath I had was in the basement of Knapp's Bakery. Atlas saw me firing the coal oven, dirty and sweating. He handed me a box from the Elevator Store with a white apron on top, telling the head baker, "Take him and show him how to run the shower." Opening the box, I found new pants, a new white shirt, my first boxer shorts, socks and shoes, one size big. At 12 years old I was going to be part of the crew up front in the cafe. Oh happy day!

Knapp's Cafe and Bakery was a 24-hour operation with 36-40 employees in the 1930s. Webster was the surgical center with an updated hospital for all of North and South Dakota and some of Minnesota. Patients had stays of 10 days to two weeks, and relatives and friends were steady customers, as were people coming and going, meeting the trains at 11 p.m. and 5 a.m., as well as freight train crews who stopped during the night. Most salesmen stayed over and ate at Knapp's, Webster being the center of density of population in northeast South Dakota.

Atlas Knapp's bakery empire crumbled to nothing more than a supporting role for his cafe operation. Not only Webster's bakeries, but all of Day County's bakeries would in one brief period go from profitable to just existing and two would become non-existing. Corporate policy and structure—their profit, greed and propaganda—wrecked the bakery business in Day County and most other places. And the general population never understood what was happening until it was too late. The service and variety of fresh bakery products were gone forever with the small town bakeries, replaced with no service, almost day-old inferior product lines at a higher selling price and profit margin. It was the small town population being ripped off by corporate structure and its policies, and it won't be the last. The bakery was just the start of big business. I will explain just how it all came about, in a very factual manner, next week—because I lived the start of big business takeover of small-town business.

33

Big business devours county's bakeries

Last week I wrote about four independent bakery businesses in Day County, using Knapp's Bakery as an example of how advanced and up-to-date they operated—employing people, spending their profits in the communities in which they lived—by paying taxes, serving the community by being mayor, school board, fire chief, etc. In one brief period in the late 1930s I would witness the downfall of independent bakery operations by big business corporate structure and policies, causing two to close shop and the remaining two reduced to supporting roles for their cafe business. Just to exist.

Bread was the profit line of the baking industry. Selling for 12 cents a loaf in grocery stores at a 20 percent profit, Knapp's Bakery was producing 2,000-2,300 loaves a week. Not for Webster alone, but 350-400 loaves a week for Aberdeen and truck loads to other towns. It was big business for Webster, employing eight people full time plus five or six part time. Flour was delivered weekly in 98 lb. bags, contracted by the ton. Lard came in 55 gallon drums.

The collapse of Knapp's Bakery business, along with all the rest, started one morning when two Sweetheart Bread trucks parked on Main Street. Out jumped four guys dressed in blue uniforms with gold buttons, white shirts, bow ties, with Sweetheart Bread across their jackets, giving away pencils and balloons.

Delivering bread to Tjelle's Store, I saw a fancy new bread rack the uniformed guy was putting up. I listened to the sales pitch he was giving Elmer Tjelle's dad, the owner. "sweetheart bread will outsell any bread. It's cheaper and you'll make 30 percent more profit. Right now you're paying too much. Ten percent more, 10 cents compared to our nine cents a loaf. Here are some pencils and balloons to give to your Sweetheart

Bread customers." When old man Tjelle said that bread rack took up too much space, he answered, "Well, now! You won't need this other rack, (meaning the one Knapp's and Hicks' was on) I'll put the money making bread up here on the top two shelves and let the other stuff have the bottom rack. Next week we will run a special. All our bread will sell for 11 cents a loaf, but your cost will not increase."

As a 14-year-old I was sold on Sweetheart Bread. The fancy uniform, bread rack, free pencils and balloons, nicely painted trucks, and Knapp and Hicks were getting rich over charging 10 cents wholesale for bread when sweetheart could sell it for nine cents a loaf.

Coming back to the bakery, two of the bakers and Atlas Knapp had a loaf of Sweetheart Bread open and were analyzing it. "Already day old, the crust is soft," one said. "Smell it. Additives to make it stay soft. And the grain (coarseness) is too smooth—it's machine made. It doesn't match our quality and it's already a day old. You can't fool people like that, can you?"

As I made my rounds to the stores, all had fancy Sweetheart Bread racks. Everyone was buying the new bread (day old) from the top two shelves, while our oven-fresh bread sat on the bottom shelf. By the third day I was hauling more old bread out of the store than I was delivering. So was Hicks. Aberdeen's Piggly Wiggly cancelled their 350 loaf weekly order, because an Aberdeen bakery was trying to compete, dropping the price two cents cheaper than Knapp could sell it. Like a new fad, everyone was buying Sweetheart. Then came the 11 cent special.

Knapp's was now baking less than 100 loaves a day. The truck route was bringing back more bread than it left with. Soon, in less than a week, the bakery was filled with 100s of loaves of day-old bread, being hauled away to Enemy Swim Church to give away. Bread sales were non-existent for Knapp's and Hick's.

Atlas knapp called a meeting. "Boys," talking to the baking crew, "you are living and seeing changing times. Small town businesses are going to be out of business. Big operations buy by the boxcar load. Profit and making money are their only concerns. I'm going to have to lay off most of the baking crew and close our truck routes. As soon as they get rid of us, (small bakeries) another big outfit will come in and they'll compete with each other." He predicted that we would see the price of bread go to 25 cents a loaf. Big business would slowly wreck small towns. Profits would go out of town, paying no taxes to support the town, doing nothing but taking local money out. "You'll all be working for them if you want a job. Small operators won't stand a chance."

Atlas said, "We are lucky we still have the cafe and will do some baking, but our profit line is gone. I've talked to Ballard Hicks. He figures he'll be locking up. I feel sorry for him and his workers, because selling his bakery equipment will not be possible. They are all going under."

It took grocery stores about three months to realize they were making less money and customers were paying more for day-old delivered bread products of inferior quality than local bakeries had produced. But it was already too late. Bristol's bakery was gone. Knapp's and Waubay were baking only to support their cafe trade. Trying to compete against Sweetheart and Old Home was too risky, because corporate structure and policies will destroy you profit wise and drive you out of business. Wholesalers love doing big volume business with big operators. Smaller orders become expensive. Bigger profits at consumer expense makes for higher prices, inferior product lines and cheaper quality.

I didn't believe Atlas Knapp 60 years ago, because big business is corporate structure— which I didn't understand. Looking at Webster today, how right he was. We had six or eight locally owned gas stations, today there is one. The bakeries are nonexistent. We have no clothing store—we had two tailors and three or four clothing stores—Nerger's, Elevator, hammerbacher's. No shoe stores, no privately owned hospital, soon there will be no independent doctors. From two optometrists, one corporate eye doctor, one part-time. From four dentists to maybe two, then only a corporate one will remain. We had a local public electrical company, now NorthWestern has all but pulled out. Our three local beer and pop distributors—all gone—combined big business. Three local creameries and Wist produce, also all consumed by big business. We had two privately owned banks, now three corporate ones.

It wasn't that these independent operators were poor managers. It was, as Atlas Knapp said, changing times and big business would take the profits and wreck small towns. Maybe I'm living a past dream, but when someone uses corporate policy for an excuse of doing business, I get real upset.

The Flying Tigers
and their ties to Webster

It was a cold fall day in 1942 when one of the biggest Webster crowds was about to welcome home a Webster boy, Robert P. Hedman, a man now called "Duke" by his Flying Tiger squadron buddies. Dressed in a suntan shirt and pants, white scarf and leather flying jacket, he now owned a flying record that no air man in the armed forces anywhere would ever surpass. Thirty-six Jap bombers and fighters shot down, more destroyed unconfirmed.

He would later explain at Joe Arbach's place (on the corner of 12th and Main where the laundromat is, which was on the Yellowstone Trail) about the Chinese writing on his jacket. If shot down they would know he was a pilot for China and they should protect him. It was also a death warrant if he landed in Japanese hands. It was called a "Blood Chit" by the Flying tigers.

Home from radio school, I was in a group listening as he talked—little of his own exploits—to high school classmates of 1935—Al Arbach, John Bregal, Art Von Rohr, LaVern Kruger, Lawrence Wattier, John Skoba. Mrs. Arbach asked Duke to sign a 4"x4" piece of cloth with carbon paper so she could stitch his name. She was making a patch quilt of all the names of boys in or going into the service. Of course Kruger, Wattier, Skoba and I signed a piece at the same time. That quilt is displayed at the VFW at times. It's got to be over 10'x10'. Two guys who signed it that night, Kruger and Skoba, died in air combat missions. As I look at the names I feel sad and lucky—remembering we signed it with Duke Hedman that night. That quilt should be preserved with the 100s of names on it.

I remember a very attractive woman, Jerri Lockwood, buying Bob Hedman a beer that night—an unheard of happening in those days. His bashful acknowledgment of a thank you to her and the laughter and rib-bing Duke would get from his close buddies.

Duke Hedman, the flying ace seven times over, told of watching one of his Flying Tiger buddies get his plane shot up, bailing out and being shot by a Jap pilot machine gun while in his parachute. Not saying who, but that Jap zero was a sure kill on the next dive. Nobody missed a word of Duke's low voice. When he talked everything got quiet in that cramped noisy tavern.

Being pressed with questions by his buddies, Duke said Christmas Day, 1941, when he got all the media write up by author Leland Stowe, a Jap's bullets hit the headrest as he bent forward in the cockpit. The headrest was full of feathers and it was like a South Dakota blizzard in the cockpit. He could hardly see the gas gauge when he landed after get-ting four bombers and two fighters. The prop stopped and he was com-pletely out of gas and ammo.

I think it was before Bob Hedman went to the Flying Tigers that he buzzed Main Street Webster. I'm sure some readers recall that Sunday morning. He was so low in that Army fighter plane he rattled every win-dow on Main Street and the churches with the roar of that fighter's engine. And he wasn't the only Webster pilot to leave his mark on Webster. Lloyd Fickler in a B-17 bomber flew over Wist Produce and dropped a crescent wrench with a note on it, which landed on the north side of Wist duck pond, south of the tracks. Also Les Knott, a pilot who was on the Doolittle raid, the first bombing of Japan, flew a squadron of B-17 bombers low over Pickerel Lake Lodge, which his mother ran. Later, telling Chuck Chilson, when asked by his flying buddies how low they should fly he told them, "Low enough to take the shingles right off the lodge." And Chilson said he remembered they just about did.

Duke Hedman had bestowed on him the highest of Chinese medals for his exploits against Japan, but was never given an american one. Because the AVG Flying Tigers was a covert secret mission set up April 15, 1941 by President Roosevelt to help China, which was at war with Japan, Army brass got no credit for the Tigers' exploits. Full authority and command went to Claire Chennault, who threw the US flying man-ual out the window and developed tactics used by WWI German flying ace, Von Richthofen, plus using characteristics of P-40-B's match up to the Mitsubishi Zero. This really rankled the Army brass, which did everything by the US book. The P-40s were fast but the Zero was more maneuverable. Dog fighting was potentially lethal for P-40s. Using a wing man (two plane team) to protect your rear was emphasized. Jap pilots were very skilled and combat experienced.

The only bright spot in the news after Pearl Harbor was the success the Flying Tigers had. The US was being defeated all over the Pacific and the Flying Tigers were now going to be put under the command of the 10th Air Force—and General "Vinegar Joe" Stillwell, who would take an army of Chinese into Burma and get his butt kicked, forced to retreat because he would not take advice or use new tactics against a combat seasoned enemy like Chennault did with the Flying Tigers. Stillwell's hostility translated into low priority to supply the Flying Tigers, and on July 4, 1942 they dissolved. Most pilots went back to their old units as flying instructors—not to fly combat again. With a record of less than 50 planes flyable at any one time against 10 to one odds, they accounted for 307 Japanese aircraft shot down, 1,500 Japanese airmen killed and over 300 planes unconfirmed with a loss of eight pilots and only six P-40s left flyable after being shot up.

Flying Tigers are America's undecorated heroes.

What crosses my mind while waiting for ducks

I'm sitting in a duck slough in the rushes on my stool, mostly enjoying nice fall weather, holding my nice new Benelli shotgun—which I told my wife would be the last shotgun I would ever want or buy. But she had heard that story three shotguns ago. The ducks weren't flying, so I was enjoying my thoughts—remembering the wooden sign on the office wall of the Holmquist Elevator. It stated that white man came to this country and saw the Indian way of life. Women did all the work—found and carried firewood, cleaned and cooked all the game and fish. All the men did was hunt, fish and eat. Where did white man ever get the idea he could improve on a deal like that? Better stop thinking like that. There's a rule at our house, you catch or shoot it, you clean it. Old times have changed.

I remembered as a kid working in the cafe, how busy we were serving all the big wheels in sports and movies who came to hunt pheasants and ducks. One opening day at 5 a.m. the cafe was packed. I was 15 years old, but had been in the cafe business for seven or eight years already. My only boss was Atlas Knapp, the owner. A cocky kid, I considered myself equal or even better than any waitress or worker. I could handle the whole counter and cash register by myself—and tell grown-up jokes to the mostly men customers at the counter. The aisle behind the counter was my stage (when Atlas wasn't there) and I remembered this one morning very clearly—opening of duck season.

Most of the talk was Ted Williams, the baseball great, who had come into Ernie Callas' cafe in the Klein Hotel the night before and had two sirloin steaks for supper. Of course, I was retorting to such talk with, "If Ted Williams wants to waste his money eating at the Greek's cafe." (That's not a politically incorrect quote, because Ernie called his cafe that and so did everyone else. Also, I'm thinking then, not now.) As all this talk about Ted Williams' supper was going on, five guys dressed in new hunting clothes and boots were laughing along with the rest of the counter customers. I continued my spiel—"If Ted Williams wanted a good steak he would eat here. He wouldn't have to order two steaks to get a decent meal." On and on my mouth was going. The counter was alive with laughter. I was center stage—pouring coffee, filling thermos bottles—when the five guys in new hunting clothes were waving at me to come to their end of the counter. Grabbing my coffee pot, I headed their way. This big, good looking guy stuck out his hand and said, "I'm Ted Williams. I'll be in for dinner and check out your steaks." The other guys sitting with him were all great players, being busy, I didn't hear them—only Ted Williams. As I took his money—he paid for all the guys with him—he said, "We'll see you tonight." A couple of guys came up to get his autograph on their hunting licenses.

I was there that night, waiting for baseball hero Ted Williams. The big back booth was set up for his group. I arranged for the best five steaks we ever cut. He arrived with his four buddies and the prettiest blonde girl. She was sort of a bump-o-de-bump type in a black and red dress. She ordered shrimp, the rest got the best porterhouse steaks ever served at Knapp's Cafe. "Kid," Williams said, "What's your name?" "Bob," I said. "Well Bob, you served one of the better steaks I've ever eaten." I thanked him, Atlas made out the bill and I got a $2 tip—big money in those 30¢ an hour days. No local customers ever tipped in those days, but it was sure payday in tips when out-of-state hunters came. Everyone— waitresses and other help worked gladly, needed or not. Help was never a problem in hunting season, because of tips.

No ducks flying, I kept remembering and wondering what happened to the autographed picture he gave me, and the other guys with him. I'm sure they were great players also. All my sources are dead, but I'm sure some old guy has to remember Ted Williams, and me shooting off my mouth. It was the talk of Main Street for at least a week after.

I wondered how many people remembered the great movie stars Clark Gable and Carrol Lombard when they hunted pheasants here. His group was about 12 people and I think they hunted one afternoon on the Parks farm. Mr. and Mrs. Fleishmann of the Fleishmann Yeast corporation were part of the group, because he checked out the bakery and gave Joe Sparrow a $5 tip for using Fleishmann Yeast—we used 50-pound boxes of it. Not to be outdone, Clark Gable went out in the kitchen and asked who made the pancakes. My mother got a $5 bill stuffed in her apron pocket. Not being a movie-goer, she felt the one-third of a week's wage tip more important than who gave it to her, and felt proud her cooking was that good. I remember all the men hunters mobbing Clark Gable for his autograph and Carrol Lombard would slip out the door. No one ever approached her. I remember seeing her in Cornwell's drug store buying face cream, a second choice—Ponds, because of the wind and sunburn. She had run out of her brand. She never appeared that good looking to me. It must have been the Hollywood makeup. both Clark and Carrol talked and acted like down home folks—no airs—in hunting clothes.

I would, a few years later at an Army air base in 1943 in Polebrook, England, run into acting chaplin assistant 1st Lt. Clark Gable. His wife, Carrol Lombard, had been killed in a plane crash, returning from a bond rally, and we would talk about pheasant hunting in South Dakota. But that's another story.

A couple of ducks started coming in. My remembering was interrupted with, "How you going to get all these old happening facts on paper to fit your column?"

Every town has to be known by something

Seventy some years ago Webster was known as "The City of Trees." The Better Webster Club used that slogan on postcards.

Driving anywhere from entering Main Street from the north to all side streets, it was like driving through a tunnel of leaves and branches. Somewhat like driving down Ninth Avenue West today.

But with new homes, businesses and recreation area construction, tree diseases this is no longer true. What made the slogan so meaningful was after the dirty 30s a real effort was made to plant trees on every farm to protect and hamper soil erosion and dust storms. The city of Webster's trees already existed and were a marvel to see.

Years later Webster was known as "The Petunia Capital of the World." Planted petunias and signs entering town proclaimed that fact. Webster Junior Chamber of Commerce sponsored that slogan.

But the one slogan that's best remembered was sponsored by Mother Nature and the Webster Sewer Department. It probably gave Webster more claim to fame and was better known throughout all the area for many years. Even up to the present time by old timers. There was a sign east of Webster on old Highway 12, known as the Yellowstone Trail, now 12th Avenue going past the swimming pool and across the golf course. The sign said, "Welcome to Webster." It was located just east of the sewer ditch bridge. Well now! About a quarter of a mile before you reached the sewer ditch you could start to smell it, even with the window up on the car. By the time you reached the welcome to Webster sign the stink was unbearable. Even on breezy days it didn't matter. The smell lingered like a cloud of foul smelling stuff coming from a freshly used outhouse somewhat mixed with the smell of an overcrowded, unventilated hog shed or sheep shed in lambin season. The sewer ditch smell could put the worst smell you can think of to shame.

By the time they reached the bridge that crossed the sewer ditch and the welcome to Webster sign most people had watering eyes. Even after you passed the bridge the smell followed you into town—on some days the whole town of Webster. When the wind was easterly the stinking smell would be the main topic of conversation. We sort of got used to it, but for newcomers it was a first impression never to be forgotten, but to be put up with.

The city fathers, after years of dredging and cleaning the ditch only made the smell worse. But they somewhat corrected it by placing a new remodeled lagoon, after the old Yellowstone Trail was rerouted north of town to its present location. But the sewer ditch still remains, and even now with spring thaws we get a faint smell that brings back memories of days past. When the wind is in the east, that's when the old guys say it's nothing like it used to be years ago. And it's no wonder to me the Jacyees wanted to improve the welcome to Webster by promoting petunias. I could write a column of those old jokes, but they wouldn't be printable.

In advertising the more of people's five senses you appeal to—sight, sound, touch, taste and smell—the more appealing the response. But the sense of smell was incorporated in the welcome to Webster sign and it outdid every known advertising campaign ever developed or remembered anywhere on the Yellowstone Trail from Minneapolis to the West Coast.

Even though any town would be embarrassed to have such a stinking welcoming as a sewer ditch entering its town from the east and leaving it from the west, Webster at its stinking best somehow prospered from its smelling entry. We had five or six grocery stores, now we have two. We had three hardware stores, now we have one. We had three great clothing and department stores, now we have none.

Our business thrived on many small farm operations and farmers. Now small diversified farms hardly exist. In those days every farm had a hog shed and a few milk cows. So that smell to them on the farm meant money. As for city slickers traveling through town, it was a disgusting, stinking smell to put up with. Most of those people spent little money in Webster businesses, but they all talked about the welcome to Webster sign and the smell at the entry of Webster, which made Webster, SD a well known place.

Somehow South Dakotans have a way of tuning the bad points people see in our state into great assets. Just mentioning Webster's smelling sewer ditch brought us free advertising—somewhat like Wall did with its miles of worthless wasteland now called the South Dakota Badlands—a nationwide tourist attraction.

I've got a lot of well-known out of state friends who don't understand small town living, but they love to hunt pheasants, ducks and geese here. Our lakes and fishing bring hundreds of out of staters here and they enjoy it. But there's something about going into a small town cafe for a local guy and knowing everybody there, talking and listening so much your coffee gets cold. I'll just say I love it here and end this column saying bad things are remembered longer than good things. But even dark clouds turn sunny most times in our towns and lives.

The greatest snow goose hunting ever

In the late 1940s and early 1950s the greatest free snow goose hunting area in South Dakota, starting about Oct. 20 of each fall, was the Sand Lake Waterfowl Refuge, located in the Hecla area of Brown County, South Dakota.

My brother Ed and our hunting buddies, Lawrence Geis and Eddie Olson had Saturday off and all week we were planning our trip to hunt at Sand Lake. Ed's hunting dog, as always, was part of our group.

In my green Plymouth station wagon we would leave Webster at midnight Friday, drive to Sand Lake to get our (and everyone else's) favorite hunting spot, Goose Corner. Getting to Sand Lake was only a 90-minute trip, but to get and hold your favorite spot meant a four-hour wait to shooting time. In below freezing weather we would sleep, talk and joke in the car—one guy always on guard to keep our spot.

Eddie Olson and Lawrence laid on the floor in the back of the station wagon covered in blankets, while brother Ed and I were up front on the trip to Sand Lake. We were 10 miles from Goose Corner when, "Bang bang! Thump thump!" I hit a big skunk. The first one to really notice was Pickles, Ed's dog, as she came bouncing up in the front seat. Then the blankets flew as Eddie and Lawrence scrambled to sit up. The skunk smell was so strong the air had a greenish tint to it. "What happened?" "We hit a skunk, can't you tell?" As all the windows rolled down, 20 degrees outside, everyone trying to find jackets, it was getting cold. But the smell lingered. Unloading the car and all our stuff at Goose Corner, it was my job to park the car, usually at the Tollefson farm about a quarter mile away. But I knew better than that. In four hours or so this area would be full of thousands of hunters ready for the goose flight of tens of thousands of snow geese leaving the refuge.

Up and down the road I drove. There were no blinds set up or parking areas like today. Thank goodness, because that stinking car in a parking area? I'm sure some 4x4 would have towed it away. Finding some brushes in the ditch I pulled down and parked it, not realizing I was only a couple hundred yards from Goose Corner. But if the wind didn't switch, come shooting time we were in great shape. Stumbling in the dark, back at Goose Corner the guys were drinking coffee and laughing about it all, building and shaping up their fence-line blinds.

It was getting light—close to shooting time. Every fence post had a hunter behind it and another waiting to take his place. As the goose flight started it sounded like WWII. Guns blazing away, geese falling. Two hunting dogs fighting over the same goose, guys yelling, "I got that one!" even though no shotgun known could shoot that far. Some guys, it's said, wore tennis shoes and never had shells in their guns were running out to pick up downed geese. Oh! the excitement! Up and down the fence line from Goose Corner as tens of thousands of snow geese flew overhead.

Meanwhile, our crew was getting our shots. Pickles was a great hunting partner for a dog, watching our gun barrels and where they were aimed. If a goose folded, out she went to get it. She knew which goose our crew shot and where it belonged.

Regardless of the Sand Lake unsportsmanship conduct of a few, it remains in the memories of all who enjoyed pass shooting geese the best pass shooting of our lives. It no longer exists, nor will it ever again. Pass and fence line shooting got a bad rap because the Game and Fish label it sky bursting—fence line slaughter. In fact, one biologist who did intern training at Sand Lake wrote a book, Carnage at Sand Lake, belittling fence line and pass shooting of geese at Sand Lake. Federal policy of refuge management, it appears, started discouraging the snow goose flight from resting at Sand Lake. And the same policy was started at the Waubay Waterfowl Refuge—saying that the large concentration of snow geese on the refuge would cause uncontrollable disease outbreaks. Rather than let fence line hunters control the overpopulation, and with no regard for the hundreds of fence line hunters from all over the state whose money had built waterfowl refuges in the first place.

Many policies were put into effect to prevent migrating snow geese from stopping and resting at Sand Lake and Waubay. Thus, no fence line hunting, no goose flight at either place. The great fence hunting became a thing of the past.

The refuges, now seeing the mistake they caused, and trying to keep their staff busy with no goose hunting, put them to work building fancy parking lots, putting up snow fence blinds—even the favorite hunting spot of hundreds of fence line hunters, Goose Corner—was turned into a handicapped parking place. It is now seldom, if ever, used.

All this not working and no snow goose flight left the goose hunter out of the picture altogether. They changed the name from waterfowl refuge, which it was intended to be years ago, to wildlife refuge. No mention of waterfowl. As for wildlife, you could never before, or now, keep wildlife out of their chosen refuge areas, managed or not. What was needed was a resting area for waterfowl and policies to attract, not distract them. If you really want to help reduce the snow goose population, go to North Dakota. As for Sand Lake and Waubay, they are not stopping. They just fly through.

Sand Lake and Waubay pass shooters and fence line hunters might have helped reduce the big overpopulation of snow geese that now exists. It's for sure the $35 a day pit hunting is not doing the job. And we better take a look at the refuge problem and policies. They are somewhat the start of this problem in South Dakota. Maybe all this talk of fence line slaughter and skybursting pass shooting, hunting for free without paying for a pit was less of a problem than the snow goose problem that exists today.

Paying to sit in a pit for a 10-20 yard shot at a goose is not the way I enjoy hunting or the way people in South Dakota should have to hunt. It's the ditch hunter, fence line hunter, pass shooter that's the true South Dakota sportsman.

Grocers preferred west side of Main Street

I often wonder why, for over 80 years, webster had only one family operated general grocery and clothing store on the east side of its three-block Main Street. That store was Nerger's grocery and clothing store (present Needs Anonymous building) operated and owned by Ed Nerger, son Eddie and daughter Grace. His son Harold died early in life in an accident. The grocery department was managed by Adolph Wickre; two high school boys after graduation worked in and serviced the clothing area, Curley Braun and his brother, Gil, who went on to establish a women's clothing chain that exists all over America today. Plus, Gil is the gent who donated half a million to build the middle school addition in Webster.

Only one east side Main Street grocery store while the west side had over a dozen operators doing business—mostly general grocery and meat markets. Not all at the same time, but at least six or seven in the same block, almost door-to-door to each other at times.

I'll start at the present Flower Cart building at Main and Fifth Avenue. From 1925-29 George Hammerbacker had a grocery and clothing store in this building. Later he started a hardware store in a building now torn down. This area has been replaced by the Head Start building.

In 1930, on April 7, Jack C. Penney was in Webster for the grand opening of his new store in the same building, J.C. Penney, Inc. After only a few years of operation a christmas time fire destroyed the contents and it never reopened for business. Many Webster area people lost layaway Christmas presents in that happening. Just ask Tina Fling—she remembers.

Next door was the Elevator Store. Chilson and son grocery and clothing store, Alfred Hagen, grocery manager. Right next door, three in a row was the old Red Owl store—grocery and meat market, Earl Walton, manager with the good looking daughters, Cella and Earline. Oh! I remember them and the good times, too! (There you go Bartos, off the story again.)

Skipping Knapp's Cafe (Day County TV now) next was McLengan's grocery and fruit market, now doc Smith's office. Next was Bailey's pool hall and bowling alley, today Todd Garry's office. Then Piggly Wiggly store, meat and grocery, Winston Hall, manager (now Hubsch's Photography). Skipping Herb Roth, Sandel, clothing and dry cleaning (the Boldes Building) now occupied by Vogl's Carpets was Ole P. Paulson grocery and meat store—where Mahlen insurance offices are located.

Now that's six grocery stores—not counting Nergers' on the east side of the street, making seven grocery operations in a half block area. Skipping up to the next block, Tjelle and son grocery and meats, where the Blossom Shoppe is today. Next door the new Red Owl grocery and meats, present day Al's Lake Area Food store. Its many past owners is another story. Next was National Tea grocery and meats, located where the vacant lot is next to Fiksdal Furniture and Gifts, which also sold groceries. Lars Fiksdal, then Al Stockstad, last being Irwin Levy grocery store. Now going to Cornwell's block. Next door was Otto Schiemmen's grocery store. Later it would be Rudy Hillgren's Red & White grocery, where Ken Roerig's insurance office is located. Now, that's a lot of grocery outlets for a small town, and that's not all. Ralph Estwick operated a grocery store in the Delaney building across from the fire station now. Also, Bauske grocery and meat market building was torn down and replaced by the Farm Store building. Curtis Hesla's Bungalow grocery was located on the corner of Main and First Street. When one operator quit another took over. There were always six or seven going at one time, sometimes more, selling groceries, clothing, shoes and fresh meat.

Well, what happened to all these general merchandising clothing, grocery and meat markets? From 1932-42 I delivered Knapp's Bakery products to all of them, except Hammerbacker's.

Most stores operated on a credit and barter system. Orders were taken and delivered, paid at the end of the month. Most farmers sold and traded fresh dressed poultry—spring chickens, ducks, geese and turkey for groceries. All stores candled eggs for cash. Home rendered lard, fruit jars of fresh cream, home churned butter was brought and bartered. No clothing, shoes or boots were sold for marked price. All were dickering items—honesty and reputation of the owner was a must. Word of mouth was the only advertising flyer.

Chain store policies of J.C. Penney, National Tea Store and Piggly Wiggly didn't last long in Webster. Nerger's, Tjelle's, Elevator Store, Fiksdal's and even Earl Walton's Red Owl did a good job of hanging in there. But when Earl died and after several new managers it existed for only a short time. Rudy Hillgren, Ralph Estwick, O.L. Paulson and McLengans left to pursue other interests. Bauske quit groceries to put more effort in meat and produce buying station operation.

Times were changing. Farmers quit raising chickens, ducks and geese. More money was being spent on the farmhouse than the barn. Working year around, milking cows sun up to dark was becoming a thing of the past for the younger operators. Bigger, faster farming methods, and so it was with the retail store business.

Refrigeration laws, food inspection, policies, federal paper laws and regulations, cash for wholesale orders, raising prices on small volume orders put credit and barter grocery stores out of business—forcing them to exist on other lines of merchandise. Nerger's, Elevator Store and Fiksdal's (Levy store) did just that—gave up the grocery business. Tjelle's hung in there—new building, new mode of operating. But the 75 hour work week was making the thought of retirement easier. The last of the old timers to go—and a new era of business was about to begin.

Shopping carts—check out gals—self-service— and cash! And that's another story.

Webster keeps two small-town groceries

I wrote about Webster having six or seven grocery stores almost door to door in a half-block area. Over a dozen different owners operated stores on main street Webster over the years, doing business with mostly farmers on a credit and barter system. Farmers, main employer of the times, slowly all disappeared as changing times reduced the farm population to about 10 percent of the many in the past years.

It all started after WWII. Young guys taking over family farms with a get up an go attitude. Expanding the farms, buying on credit, paying $100 an acre for land, big tractors, spending more money on the house than on the old barn. Young wives working in town. No chicken and egg picking for them. No milk cows. Canning vegetables was almost a lost art. Time was money. Old farmers were cash renting and selling out to big operators. Existing on 200 acres of land was already a lost cause. Get big or get out was the theme of changing times.

I'm still hearing and remembering the old guys' comments. See if any of these ring a bell. He paid more for a tractor than I did for my farm. His grain dryer is so big he can dry more grain in 24 hours then I could harvest in three years of farming. Who ever heard of raising sunflowers? Soybeans? What happened to the flax, oats, rye crops we use to raise? How long has it been since anyone used a manure spreader? It's all chemical fertilizer. Hardly ever see a guy plowing anymore. I could of bought three farms for what he's spending building that farm house. They will all go broke when hard times hit, and they are coming. (Heard that 45 years ago). Just wait—land will be selling for $30 an acre again. How can he afford to drive that new pickup? My wife used to can all of our garden stuff, cook all our own meat, raise chickens and pick eggs, raise the kids and help milk. Today young wives don't even know how to cook or make bread— they say it is cheaper to buy it. Spending money that's what it is! I'll tell you, farming is going to hell in a hand basket.

Well, the same things happening on the farm were happening to grocery stores. Old business-men were talking about young upstart store owners. The first was Bill Erickson, a Waubay boy who was a marketing manager for the Red Owl Inc. grocery stores. After years of traveling he decided Webster was the town to build a modern grocery and meat department store to fit the changing times. Remodeled a new big building for its time. A big variety of inventory. Fresh fruit display, 30 feet of meat display, fancy packaging, walls of frozen foods, three checkout counters and of course shopping carts.

All the old businessmen making statements like the old farmers. Who's going to pay all the electric bill for the lights and refrigeration? He'll be broke in a year. Who's going to use those baskets on wheels and bing, bing, bing!— that's $10.53. It's some girl you pay, not the owner like in the olden days. And he's closing at 6 p.m. and doesn't open until 8 a.m. He'll never make it.

Well, Bill Erickson made it! And so did three or four operators after him in the same location— Claire Carlson, Willie Kungel and Terry Ascher. Now another self-made grocery owner in the same location on Main Street. Allen Friesen, 24 years in grocery management and a former supervisor of a chain of grocery stores like Bill Erickson the original founder. He's the new owner of Lake Area Foods as he calls his store. Tired of traveling, he's making Webster home for his family of five. Al Friesen's store is the sole survivor of all Webster's many Main Street grocery stores of the past.

Except Mike's Jack & Jill. Let me tell you how that all that started. Located a half mile north from Al's store on a two-block square area on the east side of Main Street near the intersection of Highway 12.

Ron Hammitt started a grocery store in the present DakotaCare office building. Mike, a young carry out boy and later produce manager, was a good-looking kid filled with cheerfulness. He was friendly, fast on his feet, full of energy and pleasant to everybody with an unforgettably unique laugh.

Soon he had big dreams of building a supermarket of his own. His plan to own the very store he worked in soon came true in 1977.

Buying a swamp area, filling it in, people started to talk—that kid is crazy. He's going to put a grocery store way out there away from downtown. Nobody will go way out there for groceries. Well, said another, I don't know? It seems to me if a guy blacktops a two-acre piece of land and puts a building in the center of it, 50 cars will drive out and park around it, even if they don't know what's in it. Look at big city parking malls. People park and walk two blocks to get to the mall. But on Main Street if they can't park next to the door, they won't even stop. Times are changing.

Mike built a giant grocery store, catering to every customer's need, with a big parking lot just like the cities have. The biggest in a 50-mile area in size, with the best quality of customer service, competitive prices found in the biggest discount grocery store, plus it has a small town atmosphere only big stores dream about. In Day County everybody knows your name.

Are the two Webster grocery stores competitive? You bet they are, but in a friendly family way. Even Mike's uncle Don works for Al's Lake Area Foods.

It's fun for most of us old guys to watch a local kid learn the business from the bottom up and develop a store the big towns can take lessons from.

We may not have five or six like the olden days, but we got two that carry on the old tradition of friendly service in a modern day world of competition.

History from 1928-29, ending with a bang

Because I'm trying to beat a personal deadline, this is not a column of original stuff. I'm going goose hunting in the morning so most of this column is copied from the 1928-29 Reporter & Farmer – about three years before the dirty 30s hit Day County. Most of the people, buildings and businesses referred to are gone. But many people – relatives living here and elsewhere – might recall some memories of 60-some years ago. Of Webster the way it was and developed and contributed to the town we have today.

1928 – The year saw 16 new business establishments open in Webster and 11 new homes were erected. The only place to live was to build one.

Peabody Hospital added two more stories to its present location. Now with an 88 bed patient capacity it was the largest medical and surgical center west of the Mayo Clinic and beyond, adding more doctors to its already large staff. Dr. Walter P. Karlins, and Dr. Faris Pfister (who would spend their life careers in Webster), Dr. L.L. Collins who would replace Dr. Severeide who would move to the Pacific Coast. Also Dr. George Caldwell would open his office above Lacke Drug Store (now Cornwell Drug) and spend a lifetime in Webster.

Jan. 19 – Reporter & Farmer under new management, Mr. H. Card of Rapid City (still operates as Reporter & Farmer today).

March 15 – New clothing store opens Monday, Woodward's. R.W. Irish mgr. from Pierre leases Ebling building (now Vogl's Carpets).

April 14 – Floyd Cornwell buys Loeke Drug Store. (Floyd Cornwell served Webster as mayor and spent his lifetime in business in Webster. The drug store still bears his name today.

April 11 – The consolidated 5¢ to $1 store occupying the remodeled Lars J. Fiksdal Co. building. The remodeled store presents an attractive appearance with its two front entrances and with circular plate glass windows. This building was torn down in the late 1990s and is now a vacant lot south of Fiksdal Furniture store, after 60 years of operation.

June 10 – Webster's first aero plane arrived. Dan Carver, former owner of the Reporter & Farmer newspaper will go down in history as Day County's first aeroplane owner. It's an eight cylinder Curtis motorship of the Jenny model.

July 19 – H. Schenecker buys Liberty Theater from Blank & Deeble. Located above Security Bank, the owner of the building, which they plan to redecorate and increase the seating capacity. (It was demolished, rebuilt and is now Dacotah Bank.) Liberty Theater played an important role in Webster for over 60 years.

April 12, 1928 – Elevator Store is having a balcony built in the rear of the store. Andy Ditmanson is doing the work. (It still exists today. The building is vacant.)

May 24 – Lars J. Fiksdal dies at age 52. A prominent Webster merchant for over 30 years, Fiksdal's store still bears his name.

June 21 – Local merchant laid to rest. Resident since 1912, Albert Frank Vawrinek opened a tailor shop in Brooks building. He leaves five children, Alberta 14, James 12, Frank 10, Anna six and John four. Only John, a 1942 classmate is still living today. He is retired, but a very impressive man of accomplishments.

Aug. 6 – Red Owl opens store in Webster. Earl Walton, Mgr. (Now Golden Age Center.)

Aug. 6 – Baily poolhall moves into new building. (Now G. Todd Garry, PA location.)

Sept. 13 – Rev. John Kildahl will succeed Rev. F. Schmidt, St. John's Lutheran Church.

Dec. 13 – New county agent, Alfred O'Connel takes over Jan. 1, 1929. (Al O'Connel served Day County for the rest of his life.)

Sept. 13 – The rooms beneath the Security Bank have been fitted up in apple pie order and now occupied by three couples of newlyweds. They are Mr. and Mrs. Clarence Grue, Mr. and Mrs. Eddie Peters and Mr. and Mrs. Warren Lakin. The three cooing couples are preparing a dainty little sign which will inform an observant public the place will hereafter be known as Honeymoon Flats.

All of the newly mentioned happenings in 1928 and people, businesses survived the dust storms and depression of the 1930s. And the doctors and businesses became a very important part of Webster's development as long as they existed from the great times to the dirty 30s depression and 40 years after. But the people of 1928 were really a tough breed. And having heard of a couple of gun shot accidents, one which a close friend from Grenville was involved in, I copied this gun shooting story from Nov. 14, 1929 Webster Journal, written by Will Wells, the editor, whom I knew well and bought his home after he died. I think the Game and Fish boys and my friend Jerry Lesnar will enjoy along with the other readers who might be bored by now.

Nov. 21, 1929 – Shot a game warden (headline)

GAME WARDEN AUGUST Jenson of New Effington and well known is this county received a badly burned face and scalp wound when Rinke Dykstra of Rosholt fired a 410 gauge revolver into the warden's face Friday when Jenson arrested three Dykstra boys and William French for shooting muskrats. The shooting occurred about 3:30 o'clock p.m. in the afternoon about a mile west of mud lake near Rosholt. Jenson had watched the party shooting muskrats for some time through his field glasses, when the Dykstra boys and their hired man, William French decided to quit. Jenson accosted them and attempted to search Rinke Dykstra, the oldest of the boys. Jenson held Dykstra in his left hand by the front of his shirt and searched him with his right hand. When the search was partially completed the alleged offender drew the revolver from his clothes with his right hand and shot into Jenson's face. The latter saw the movement and pulled his head to one side, the bullet striking him on the cheekbone and glancing, but he received a badly burned face and nasty wound.

All of the party, Rinke Dykstra finally being subdued with the butt end of a gun, were arrested and taken to Sisseton. George and Henry Dykstra were fined for shooting rats and released, while Rinke Dykstra will appear before Judge Babcock at the next term of court. Archy Ellington of New Effington was with Jenson at the time but was too far distant to lend his aid.

Of woolen underwear and sheepskin coats

It's too hot to write, certainly too uncomfortable to read. That's my excuse. But it's never too hot to golf. At least that's what my wife tells me.

To make matters worse, my air conditioner ran out of the stuff that cools the house. Got that taken care of real quick, thanks to Jim Gollnick. Then the water bill came, and that did it. I haven't watered the lawn, nobody in the house had diarrhea, no excess flushing. Yet it was about 30 percent higher than I ever paid.

It brought back a lot of old memories of my grandpa. He was old ever since I was a kid. No water, no electricity, no air conditioning and few windows. As I remember him, he had a life style all his own and he and Grandma were happy and content with it. A lot of habits I'm glad I didn't inherit and a few I hope I did. And I'm about to tell you why.

Grandpa Fred A. Brooks was born somewhere in Scotland in 1852. He met and married Jane R. Punket, born in England in 1859. They settled in Iowa until it got too crowded, then headed north to South Dakota. He staked a claim on a quarter of land beside a couple of Indian trails. This was the 1870s, before railroads. He thought he was in the middle of nowhere, not realizing he had located in what would become a high traffic area. Some years later, Sam Brooks established a cafe known as Brooks' Corner on Highway 12 and old Highway 81 on the northwest corner of his homesteaded quarter about three miles west of Summit.

Getting back to my story…First the railroad cut through Grandpa's land going south of his tar paper shack about 150 yards. He wouldn't move the shack and was very upset about it. But he forgot all his disadvantages and got a job with his team of mules. Grandma carried cold spring water to the workers. In exchange they got a lot of lumber to improve their homestead. Also, excess piles of coal and wood were somehow gotten from grateful workers. As late as 1940 Grandpa never had to buy coal. He would go along the track and pick up his winter supply. I remember the old tar paper house just shook every time a train passed by, but it never bothered Grandpa or Grandma—day or night.

Later it would be the Indian trail to the north, which would become the Yellowstone Trail cutting across the north part of his homestead which would upset Grandpa. But the last insult to his homestead was when the Indian trail from Watertown to Highway 12 became Highway 81 on the east side of his house, less than 50 yards away from his original shack, which he would not move.

Now Grandpa was really upset, but worse things were to come. I think it was in the 40s, 60 years after he came to South Dakota. Now in his 80s, Grandpa had to move his original shanty because they were going to build an overpass over the railroad. The building crew felt sorry for them as they were moved to their son's farm until the bridge was completed. Grandpa told the powers that be, "I want that house put back just like it was when you moved it," but the bridge crew dug a cement basement and put in new windows and doors when they replaced it. Upon his return, he had a conniption fit because he wanted his house back on the dirt ground—not on a basement. The crew gently moved the shack off the basement and filled it with dirt to satisfy the stubborn old Scotsman. No one understood his actions.

Grandpa Brooks' only transportation was a four wheel buggy, one iron wheel and one wooden one in the back, pulled by an old mule, as late as the 1930s. It was a rickety outfit that made bi-monthly trips to Slaathaug's grocery store in Summit. I remember one of those trips, when my brother and I spent a week's vacation there. We sat in back on the wooden buggy seat with a cream can and case of eggs that would be traded for flour, sugar and salt. We took the trail alongside the railroad tracks because gravel and cars on Highway 12 affected old Jack, the mule. Highlight of the whole trip, which took all day, was we got to ride old Jack home because there was no room for us in the buggy with the empty cream can, egg case and groceries.

I also remember the nights—getting up at daybreak, eating Grandma's pancakes made from scratch with real buttermilk left over from the churn.

Grandma made cottage cheese and butter using a crock butter churn and wooden plunger. There was always fresh whipped cream, eggs, ham, bacon, side pork and gravy. She used honey for sugar. There was fresh lettuce—not head type you buy in the store, but leaf type from the garden, served with a real cream, sugar and vinegar sauce on it. Grandma was a great cook on her wood fired kitchen stove. Pan fried chicken and gravy, fresh garden vegetables. I've never eaten vegetables as good as she fixed them. No measured stuff for Grandma. A pinch of this, a dab of that. No recipes, it was all in her taste and head. Her cooking is a lost art.

Grandpa liked homemade horse radish, which Grandma and us kids hated. I believe they lived to eat because there was nothing else but farm work. No hunting, fishing, golf or bowling. Just work.

Grandpa had a life style all his own with a lot of what I considered bad—which I hope I didn't inherit. And some of his life style I hope I did. He was only five feet tall. I got some of that shortness. He was a hard worker, a very fair man. But when things changed his landscape he couldn't cope with that. I hope if my lifespan goes on I can adapt to change better than he did.

Old Grandpa Brooks wore woolen underwear all summer long. He said he lived in South Dakota over 70 years and that was the best way to tolerate 90-100 degree days. He washed his feet every night, never changed underwear and seldom took a bath. Yet I don't recall him stinking to high heaven. To make matters worse, on real hot days—raking hay in August—he wore a sheepskin coat when it really got hot to keep the heat out. He told us it works. No way, we reasoned! Years later mentioning this to others, they said, "Sure, my grandad did the same thing." However, no one could recall the sheepskin coat bit.

Grandpa died in 1957 at age 105. Grandma died in 1955 at age 96. Both are in the Brooks family plot in Webster Cemetery.

Neither of my grandparents went to church, but each night they read the Bible by lamplight. Grandma would often sing hymns. Grandpa would hum Jesus Loves Me. I never heard Grandpa cuss or use bad talk to farm animals or anyone else. He had a lot of patience with us wild grandkids—teaching us to play checkers and snare gophers.

They seemed very old people to us kids. And when I drive past Brooks corner on Highway 12 I remember them. Nothing remains—not even a foundation. But I can take you to the spot where the spring well was located. I remember helping my uncle dig up a rusty can so many paces from the well. It contained an old sock with $2,500 in it, moldy five, 10 and 20 dollar bills in it. Grandpa wanted to pay for his funeral. He died three days later, an old pioneer. Self supporting South Dakotan to the end.

The bone collectors of the dirty 30s

It's been over 60 years since I've seen or heard from a most-remembered boyhood friend, Arlie Floren. He was one of the kids in our gang who worked hard, played hard and could deal with trouble. Now 80 years old and retired, a man of great accomplishments in the mechanical auto parts field with a Ford Motor dealership. He's not quite as well known as his brother, Myron of Lawrence Welk fame, but just as respected in his field of expertise as Myron is in his great accordion accomplishments. And it's his letter to me after a story I wrote about fun times on his motorcycle back in the early days that I'll be telling you about.

I quote from Arlie's letter, "Do you remember the following? Shortly after moving to Webster (1936) I became acquainted with you and either one or two of your brothers. There was a market for old bones and you made a deal with Tjelle to pick up bones around their slaughter house. You had a trailer and maybe no car, as I furnished the car to pull the trailer. There was no license on the trailer. We sold the bones and were nearing your house with the empty trailer. We saw police chief Dougherty in his Model A pursuit car closing in on us. We unhooked the trailer and by hand and foot pushed it to your house. I don't remember how we divided the spoils, but would guess that we used more gas than we got for the bones. Well, make a little or lose a little. It's the volume that counts.

"P.S. – Webster and Day County had and probably has the cutest girls!"

Well now! Arlie old boy! Arlie Floren never had a problem dating any Day County girls. You were a fun guy and a boyhood friend I'll never forget! You had some pretty good-looking sisters, too! One became a homecoming queen in Sioux Falls after they moved there.

I got off track with your mentioning girls. I recall some of those memories also, but getting back to the bones story.

Back in 1936-40 no grown ups, parents or anyone else had money. Most young workers were working for room and board, just existing. If us kids wanted movie money, an ice cream cone or a yo-yo – all luxury items – it was after we bought the necessities – shirt, overalls and shoes. We had to find a way to make money. Farm kids could trap muskrats. Town kids sort of followed their lead, trapping muskrats along the railroad rights-of-way, picking wool off fences of farms that had sheep, snaring gophers and selling tails for bounty, climbing trees and stealing crows' eggs and young for bounty, going to the city dump with a magnet and picking up scrap copper, aluminum, brass, pop and beer bottles. And raiding every trash pile from Seventh Ave. (known as Codfish Ave. where the so called rich people lived). Codfish Ave. got its name from Boston salted codfish wooden boxes that was a staple food item for midwest families. And the Boston company was a well known wealthy family.

All the trash piles Eighth-Tenth Ave. were known as Plunger Ave. because all the new houses were mortgaged to the max – by new upcoming businessmen. I don't recall any rich kids. It seems all of us were poor kids – ambitious, hard working and full of mischief. Anything to make a dime.

One of the most respected men we knew was a scrap, junkyard man, Louie Rohde, who we sold our salvage copper, brass and stuff to. Then we found out you could still sell old bones. This was a virgin business area that had been long forgotten. Less than 50 years back from 1937 the prairies of Day County were covered with wildlife. Buffalo, oxen, horse bones – every farmstead had heaping piles of bones that had to be cleared from the fields before they could be broken and planted, much like rock piles of today being used for riprap. Enterprising entrepreneurs of past days found a market for them to be ground up and used as fertilizer, glue and mixed for livestock food supplement. The bones were shipped out by train carload and most piles disappeared.

Rather than fight the competition of all the other kids in the dump and rich people's trash piles, I thought we hit a gold mine idea in bones. Every farm had a buffalo skull hanging on the barn and a small bone pile. In fact, the Storley farm at Roslyn had a spring creek in which lots of buffalo bones were found. And dry lakes of Waubay, Rush and Minnewasta were producing quantity finds of bones. No one was selling them until Louie Rohde told me he would buy them. As a kid, time, labor and work meant nothing. It was volume and money we got that was profit. Only thing with bones, you had to sell by the ton – not a couple hundred pounds as we kids tried to do.

The kids in our band mostly ended up in the WWII thing. We did very well with our high school educations. Some of us, like Arlie and me, didn't make a lot of money but we sent our kids to college and enjoyed the life of family and things we missed out on growing up. We got most of the joys and toys and good things in life. Now 80 plus years old, knowing we were the best at what we did because of being brought up in hard times in South Dakota, we are pretty content. As for our childhood, it was fun – never boring. We never felt a better life existed until we lived it, because everything from 1936 wasn't like before and getting better every day we live.

I enjoyed recalling the old bones story – and of course the p.s. part of the letter about cutest girls. Which for both of our sakes I omitted. But I will add, Arlie Floren always had a car or some kind of transportation. And do you recall – or maybe want to forget – two Roslyn cheerleaders we dated in the back seat practicing their cheers? One went something like this:

Lutefisk and lefse, Copenhagen snoose;
Come on boys, we're yelling for you, we're yelling like the duce.
Roslyn, Roslyn, Roslyn!
A lot more of this could be said, but not written.

I was reminded of this bones story once before, when Bill Kanago found a couple of buffalo skulls in Waubay Lake in 1980. He sold them for $25 apiece!

So us kids had the right idea – we just sold them too soon.

Thanks for a great memory, Arlie.

Ice fishing has changed from the old days

My wife remarked, You've been spending too much time goose hunting. I'm glad it's over. It's the holiday season write something in keeping with Christmas and New Year's. Snowman, jingle bell type stuff. Not all this old man and old time stuff.

Well now! Santa is an old guy. Christmas is an old-time tradition. Santa used to come by sleigh and reindeer. Now it's by helicopter and airplane. Old-time gifts used to be popcorn balls and new underwear at our house. Today it's expensive video toys and maxed out credit cards.

That said and after being called an old grinch I'm going to write my column my way. And I'm not going to let my wife read it.

Years ago the main fall project was readying the fish shack for winter fishing. Making sure all the inside lines and iron coal and wood burning stove and pipes were cleaned. Table and chairs and outside lock were in place. Gas light had new mantels. The shacks were so big and heavy getting them on the ice and off was a full day's work. Once located on the ice they seldom moved until spring. They were placed in clusters of 20-30 shacks like little neighborhoods on the only two fishing lakes near Webster. Mostly Enemy Swim and Pickerel.

Most of the fishing was done after work in those days from 6 p.m.-midnight weekdays. Crappies, walleye and a few northern and perch. And just as important as bait was lunch. Every shack had a pot of coffee and can of water boiling baloney or wieners. And there was always a card game going on in every other shack. Whist and pinochle and of course there were poker players also. Because a lot more time was spent waiting for the fish to bite. Then when they bit the fun really began. When you had a good hand of cards everything stopped because a cork went down and a fish was caught. Card game rules were many and varied. When the fish started biting everyone would get confused over the rules, breaking up the game.

If you really wanted the fish to bite, just make yourself a sandwich. Sure enough, most of it would be lost trying to set the hook on a line going down.

I don't recall a lot of beer drinking mostly coffee. But there was always a bottle of brandy or peppermint schnapps appearing to celebrate the trophy walleye someone would catch.

Fishing on the ice was great! Drive to the lake, unlock the shack door, build a fire in the stove, open the holes, put the lines down, visit and play cards and have coffee with all your local friends. And when the fish started biting it was a joy for everyone in ice shanty town.

But ice fishing of the past changed. First, small iron stoves were hard to fine and oil and propane heaters replaced them. Then ice chisels were hard to come by and electric ice augers started to show up. Gas lanterns were being replaced by battery and electric bulbs. Then wheels that raised and lowered the shacks made them moveable. The ice shack neighborhood was no longer a stable unit it moves in all directions all over the lake. And the worst was yet to come as ice fishermen became more lazy and rich.

What used to keep guys from chiseling new holes in ice 30 inches thick can be done in 10 minutes with gas ice augers. Quiet times ice fishing are gone. The roar of snowmobiles, four wheelers, ice augers drilling holes. Portable fish houses that set up in minutes, portable gas heater, electric fish finders, no room to cook inside, no card playing, no neighborhood. Everyone moving, setting up, taking down, drilling new holes. Nobody knows the guy fishing next to him. It's a rarity just to see a local guy you know. License plates from every other county and state fishing everyplace. But the two lakes, Pickerel and Enemy Swim the only lakes years ago are now considered third class fishing spots. It seems every new slough has fish in it. And it's a good thing too, because the ice no matter how thick couldn't hold the increase in ice fishermen now fishing in our area.

One thing for sure, ice fishing will never be the same as it was years ago. So for Christmas, Santa, I'll need a four wheeler or snowmobile, a portable fish shack and sled to put it on, in ice fish location and depth finder and a hard working fishing buddy to help me set it up. And some of those new fangled ice fishing rods and reels. And a gas heater and gas ice auger and new trailer to haul all of it.

On second thought, skip it Santa. Because I'm too old to spend my time setting up and taking down all that new fangled stuff. I'll just take my old fish sticks in a five gallon pail and enjoy fishing like I always have. But maybe a gas operated ice auger would be a good thing to have as my old ice chisel is dull and worn.

One more thing, Santa. Bring my wife a new vacuum cleaner because she enjoys housework more than ice fishing. And if you do, Santa, we're both in trouble.

Peace on earth and happy holidays, everyone.

The birth of the Webster golf course

Webster golf began with an organizational meeting July 14, 1927. About three dozen businessmen kicked in about $10 apiece, men like L.W. Bicknell, Frank Mohs, Rich Fiksdal, Dr. Cook, Dr. Deeble, the Drs. Peabody, E.A. Sewell, Floyd Cornwell, H. Chilson, Ed Nerger, E.A. Locke and many more. The big pushers were W.C. Happe and his son Grant, owners of Webster Candy Kitchen. They bought 80-plus acres of land—slough, rocks and buffalo grass, about two and one-half miles southeast of Webster. By April 19, 1928 Grant Happe let contracts to his dad to draw up and lay out an improved nine-hole sand green golf course. F. Welch was employed as caretaker and green fees of 50 cents were set for non-members. An Aug. 15, 1928 Reporter & Farmer quoted, "Webster can now boast one of Northeast South Dakota's finest golf courses.

July 18, 1929, Art Lundquist got Webster's first hole-in-one. It was on number six, 180 yards, par three. Ed Locke got the second hole-in-one in 1930 and no records appear after that. First northeast conference high school golf tournament, held at Britton, was won by Webster's Milo Hein in 1933. A trophy was presented to the high school Oct. 9 that year.

Those days, golf clubs had wooden shafts and leather strip grips. It wasn't uncommon to see an iron head go flying off after a shot. They also had trouble with leather grips unraveling. Oiling and care of clubs after every round was mandatory. Greens were small, filled with fine sand mixed with oil to keep it from blowing away. An iron drag was used to make a path to the hole for putting. Golf bags were mostly heavy leather. Everyone walked—no carts or pull-type either. The good golfers used kids for caddies to carry the bag, clean the sand and oil off the ball after putting. Like today they had spike golf shoes. Unlike today, knickers were part of the outfit. Even a white shirt and tie were part of the game and rules. No fancy Webster clubhouse. Just an old wooden shack, which was moved to Webster after the old golf course was sold.

Golf clubs of yesterday had names. Like mid-iron, brassie, spoon mashie. Today, other than the driver, golf clubs are called by numbers and wedges of all degrees. Most everyone rides a golf cart or pulls one. Only the brave would wear knickers, white shirt or tie. Today, shorts and tennis shoes. Dress is no longer part of the game. Caddies on the local course are a thing of the past also. Few places exist today with sand greens. Golf equipment has been upgraded today. Steel and graphite shafts and lightweight metallic heads have replaced wood shafts and wooden heads. Golf shoes were the last to change—from steel to plastic spikes. Webster produced some of the best golfers and still does. Enough history.

Let me tell you what a golf afternoon and evening was really like in the old days. Most of our teachers, strict and respected were golfers. Herb Hartshorn, Frank Gellerman, Coach Welch, all highly respected, role models, businessmen, never seen in a bar. Pillars in the church and community—except at the old golf course. Only a chosen few caddies were used on golf day. Virgil Fick, Baldy Schlamann, myself, LaVern Krueger and a very young Carroll Peterson. We had fulltime jobs but somehow managed to be at the golf course on golf day. I'll never forget, nor will any of the others, Frank Gellerman and Grant Happe's little talk as they told us very manly and frankly, "What you see and what's done here, what you hear here, we all leave here. We don't talk about it to anyone. If this rule or code is broken you won't ever be welcome back here." A talk like that to this group of street-wise roughies, which we were, made us feel trusted and accepted by club members. We were top caddies. We were paid well, treated with pop and food. We got to go to other towns all over South Dakota and Minnesota in nice big cars and got help getting off our regular jobs on tournament Sundays. And we were not going to upset a deal like that by shooting off our mouths. We never laughed at a bad shot and never called any club member by his first name. It was always Mr.

Well, what went on golf night at the old golf course. A tub of beer was placed on holes three and six. And one at the club shack. It was a jolly, happy time. Everyone was laughing and joking—no business talk allowed. It was fun for us caddies inside, but not showing on the outside, to see a stern, strict school teacher like Herb Hartshorn become a joking laughing guy. And the nicknames Grant Happe (who I caddied for) gave and called some of the members. And the remarks and cussing done on badly hit balls. The bets of 50 cents a hole—big money. Our surprise at who made them. Good losers and bad.

When golf play was over Dr. Karlins was grilling steaks. The first charcoal grill I ever saw used a big cut down wash tub with a wire grill over it. He would grill 10 steaks at a time and pour his sauce of garlic and butter over them. My job was to place lettuce salad and baked potato on the plate—and be sure the well done and rare got to the right members, who by now had switched from beer to the better cocktail stuff. Soon lanterns were lit and a couple of poker tables set up. Mostly dime and nickel— high stakes at the other table with a lot of cigar smoke now by guys who never smoked anywhere else. After cleanup us caddies went home, never to talk about things like the teasing Mr. Hartshorn was getting about the music teacher, Miss French, who he would later marry. It shocked everyone in Webster—except us caddies. We also knew what member was having the next baby and what man was marrying who.

The early golf members worked hard and made things happen without help from the city, state or government. If they thought a golf course was needed they built it. If they needed a skating rink they flooded a lot. If we needed a library they didn't wait for Andrew Carnegie to give Webster one. They arranged for one. If the school board needed a candidate they provided a couple. They were the leadership. One thing about the old golfers and leadership. Neither would have amounted to much if they didn't work hard and play hard.

Golf and the many lame excuses for it

It was the first nice day in May as I heard her say, "A pretty lame golf excuse." I was being straightened out after coming home from an afternoon of golf when I should have been mowing the lawn, spraying dandelions and putting fresh dirt in her flower bed. And the screens should have been put on a week ago.

Then I said, "This retirement stinks. I wish I could go back to my corporate job just to get some rest and relax!" I should never have made that statement to her. Getting myself in deeper, "And I wasn't just playing golf. I was paying my civic rent, sort of." As she stood there listening and staring at me, trying to be nice, I said, "You know dear, it takes a lot of things to make a great town. Good ball parks, a swimming pool, an airport, library, tennis courts—and they all cost the city money. But the most used place of all is the golf course, and the least expensive to operate because it pays for itself. And I'm doing the city a favor by supporting it." And I shouldn't have said that either. She stopped me right there.

"Sit down, dear!" she said. "I'm going to explain just how expensive your golf support is. Do you realize it costs you $1 a hole in green fees on weekends? For a good golfer that's almost 23 cents every time he swings at the ball." "Yeah! That's a good young golfer. I'm an old golfer—I shoot a score of 50, not 40. I miss a lot of shots. I get my money's worth." "Do you?" she says. "Shooting a score of 50, every swing you take at that golf ball cost you 18 cents."

"Wow," I said. "You sure know your math—but not golf. I'm a member of the club. I don't pay green fees!" "Oh don't you? Membership, one person $159, handicap card $13, golf cart rental space $63.60 for a total $235.60. How many rounds do you play in a 120 day season? Hot, windy and rainy days—maybe 40 rounds. That's almost $5.90 a round, almost 12 cents a swing of your club at the ball, hit or not for an old 50 score golfer."

After all that, like a bent nail, I was straightened out and driven to work—kind of enjoying the purr of the lawn mower. But I knew I was going golfing the next day with my old guys foursome.

Next day, sitting in the clubhouse having a drink with my old golfing buddies, old Fred said, "I'm going to trade my old golf cart in on a new club car, $3,300 to boot. I got a great deal on a fancy club car." Yesterday all came back to me—how expensive golf was. I wondered how Fred could explain that. "Fred," I said, "do you know it costs us old guys almost 12 cents every time we swing a club at that golf ball, hit it or not?" Old Fred just grunted and said, "At our age we need all the exercise we can get and playing golf is good exercise. Riding in the golf cart just makes the exercise a little more comfortable. Look, a guy 101 years old just broke the oldest player to get a hole in one record. And the last record holder was 99 years old. Boys, we got a lot of golf to play ahead of us. Bring us another round, waitress. You know, boys, golf is cheaper than a round of drinks, even in a small town place like this," as he laid out his money for drinks and a tip.

Off Fred goes again! "You guys, it's a lot cheaper playing golf than paying $50 for a little bottle of heart attack pills like the guys who don't exercise and play golf like we do. That's what I tell my wife. Golf is my way of saving on heart attack pills." "Yeah, Freddy, riding in a new fancy golf cart—that's exercise?" "You bet. Golf exercise in comfort!" Fred says. "And another thing, laughter don't hurt either. It prevents lung croup and asthma. Let me tell you, there was this old guy's wife who was really on him about love. She said, 'If I died I suppose you would get married again.' He told her if he did it would be a baldheaded woman because every time he wanted to go somewhere all he ever heard was, 'Look at my hair! I can't go like this!' 'Quit talking like that,' the wife said. 'I'm serious. If you married again I bet you would let her wear my fur coat and jewelry.' He assured her he would not. 'I bet you would let her use my golf clubs!' 'No! I would not! She's left-handed.'"

That's an old one, Fred! "Yes, but we're old guys. I can't remember the new off colored funny ones the young ones tell and some of those young flat bellies were too young to know our old jokes. Then there was this guy who couldn't see too well, hitting at the golf ball. He hit the dirt behind it, along side of it—tore up the turf missing the ball with every swing. When the leader of all the ground insects ordered his troops to get on the ball. 'It's the only safe place in the area!'"

With that, I was about to leave the clubhouse. Old Fred promised no more jokes, but wasn't going to give up on why he needed a new golf cart. "Guys, do you realize two-thirds of our golf membership is over 60-75 years old? And older! Men and women shoot 47-50 scores. The other one-third shoot in the lower 40s. It costs them 18-20 cents a shot! Those young flat bellies working hard for a living are the ones I feel sorry for. They bang that ball over 250 yards and I don't think it's their new golf equipment either."

"No, Fred. We think somewhere over the years your banging powder got a little damp. If it takes two drives to equal one of the young guys', learn to live with it. That's part of our golf game now." And one thing never changes over the years in golf. That's the lame golf excuse. Which was proven as I visited with a corporate friend at his office, surrounded by busy secretaries. His executive son approached and said, "I've got to leave at 2:30. I've got an appointment with Dr. Titlist." "Sure, go ahead son!" I had a clouded look on my face. Titlist, same name as the golf balls I shoot. My old corporate friend, in a whispered voice, said "He's got a 2:30 tee time." We both smiled, hoping the working secretaries didn't understand. The son had just made a lame golf excuse.

I also wondered if he might get straightened out by his wife or live-in, as the case might be in this changing world, when he got home for some chores he had failed to do. The game of golf will always be played, using a lame golf excuse. The green's too hard. It's the wind…the ball…the club that affects the score. Not the personal elements of work or wife. Golf has its place and time doesn't matter to young or old as lame golf excuses live forever.

How a C+ project landed me my first job

Today it's one of those South Dakota weather days—cold, wintery, snow piled up beyond a normal guy's butt, way up to his armpits. And I'm depressed and housebound, thinking old man thoughts. Like what could have been—what should have been—and of all things, how lucky I've been.

Remembering my first real job—the one I got on my own—no, not the one I grew up with at Knapp's Cafe in the late 20s and 30s. That job was sort of like chores. Not much take-home pay, just plenty to eat and a warm place to work. More of a growing up experience than a job. With no future, and besides, I'd be in the army in a few months.

It was my last year in high school (1942). The assignment in typing class was to create and type a letter to a future employer. Address the envelope. The teacher suggested it should be to a corporate company and gave us make believe addresses and form letter examples. And I needed to get a good grade to pass this course—I was on the borderline of graduating. I'm not good at make believe. To me this letter had to be real, and the only person I knew about was my dad's big railroad boss, vice president L.B. Porter of Chicago-Milwaukee-St. Paul and Pacific Railroad—a man my dad would guide pheasant and duck hunting when he came to Webster with his friends in his big personal railroad coach car.

This typing assignment was a week-long project, in which I stated my dad was a railroad signal man and I was applying for a job like his. My experience was, I could tie wire, climb poles (I had worn out most of the telephone poles in our back alley practicing climbing using Dad's worn out spikes and belts) and had watched my dad drill rails, insert channel pins while bonding track and so on. After spending hours after school typing it, my teacher was not impressed. I got a C+. Taking the letter home, I thought, "If I can erase that a C+ and mail that letter." I thought I did a great job of erasing the C+, and mail it I did. This was in April of 1942. I'd be 18 in the fall anyway—in the army. So what! Maybe I could impress my dad with at least a rejection letter with L.B. Porter's address on the outside of it. Wouldn't that be nice. A letter addressed to me from L.B. Porter, vice president of the railroad Dad worked for and a man he regarded with high esteem.

Sure enough, about a week later, after school my mother said, "Bob, what's L.B. Porter writing to you about? Have you been playing around the depot? What have you done?" I couldn't wait to tear open the letter. In it was a temporary railroad pass, to proceed to Stevens Point, WI. Report May 11 to the foreman of a signal crew. Starting wage 78 cents an hour, 50 hour work week. That's $39 a week. I'm rich! Most grown men weren't making that in a month. Mother was crying and Dad was very proud, telling me what I should do and not do when joining the crew—and how lucky I was. And I couldn't wait to show that letter to my teacher the next morning—the results I got from her C+ grade.

Then the trouble began. Frank Gellerman, school superintendent, called me to his office and told me my grades weren't good enough to graduate yet and I couldn't miss two weeks of school to take this job. But he said it was a great offer. I'd better talk to Atlas Knapp (my school job boss, also on the school board). This I had not done.

Well, to shorten the story, Atlas said, "Bob, there's no way you could ever make that kind of money around here. I hate to see you go, but good luck." Frank Gellerman arranged for me to take a crash course in English, which I was failing, early tests in other subjects and on May 9 shook my hand and gave me my diploma. My only regret would be the speech I would have given as president of the senior class at our graduation.

I got on the train and reported to the signal crew, about as far away from home as I had ever been. The foreman was a tough, ape-like built guy who said he knew my dad. I was assigned a bunk in the sleeping car, stowed my stuff and assigned as a helper to the local signal maintainer, cutting tree limbs over a 4,400 volt line in the area.

It was my second week in the crew. I was about to get initiated.

After supper the crew gathered outside our bunk cars in the rail yards of Stevens Point, WI. The foreman said, "Bartos, you've been pretty good at going up and down those 16-foot line poles without your safety belt. Now, I want to see how good you are using one. Get your spikes and belt on. These poles are 80-foot yard poles. Watch me." Up the pole he went. He leaned back in his safety belt, took out his jack knife, stuck it in the top of the pole and down he came. "OK, Bartos, get my knife."

All the crew helped me adjust my belt and get started. Up I went, no problem. I made it to the top. Grabbing the knife, I folded it and looked down. I froze. My knees started to tremble.

I could hear laughter from the crew on the ground and the foreman on the ground barking to the crew, "Shut up! Bartos, lean back in your safety belt. I'm coming up." He had me take my left leg loose and jam the spike in at an angle. Slowly, one step at a time, I walked on down. "Keep your head up." I expected the worst when I got to the ground. There was only silence when the foreman asked if any of the other guys wanted to try that 80-footer. Nobody said a word. Even in my failure I was accepted—because other than the foreman, nobody ever got to climb an 80-footer. It became a standard joke, when someone got cocky or mouthy, to say, "I wonder if he doesn't need a shot at an 80-footer to cool him off." Well, at least I got to the top of one—even if I had to be walked down.

What a dumb thing to think about on a cold snowy day. Your first job and the 80-foot line pole. Oh well. At least I spent a couple of hours remembering and the wind has let up. I think I'll do something productive—like go have coffee with the old guys.

The first biggest
fish I ever saw

Do you remember the first big fish you ever saw? The first fish I remember was a big black bass, caught on a fly rod by Bub Ross of Waubay at Pickerel Lake. He brought it to the lodge to show it off back in the 1930s. There were no fancy spinning reels or rods in those days. Few level wind reels. Fly rods were common. Most fishing was done from shore with cane poles and real cork bobbers—no plastic red and white ones like today.

There were some flat bottom wood boats propelled by oars and a few ritzy cedar strip boats. A few one-lung fishing boat motors which took more effort to keep running than time spent fishing. And most fish caught were by still fishing—bullheads, crappies, bluegills and perch. Then came six-horse Johnsons and Evenrudes and some off brands like Atwater.

Trolling was started by old-time fishermen like France Hallstrom, Frank Dickinson and Guff Hawkinson using triangle rigs with a weight and leader and a Maps spinner or Prescott Pike spinner tipped with a minnow. Also, trolling was done using a Dare Devil, red and white Bass-O-Reno, jointed creek chubs and other spoons and plugs. As I remember, casting with many new type anti-backlash reels, none of them worked. Bird nesting the line in a mess, which took hours to untangle. I will never forget the first spinning reel to come into Webster—a big clumsy plastic ball enclosed with a glass type rod in the 1940s. You could cast 50 or 60 feet. No backlash. It worked perfect. In fact, I still have one. Then came the open face and enclosed face spinning rods, much like the improved models we use today.

And everything in boats, motors and tackle took off after what seemed like a hundred years of old-time fishing. Fishing all of a sudden became a $20-30,000 investment in the 1990s. In the 1930s catching a six-pound walleye was show off time—today it's just another fish on the stringer.

There were only two good walleye and northern pike fishing lakes known by me—Pickerel and Enemy Swim. The rest were considered pan fish lakes. Most were very shallow or dry—that's not the case today. They are better fishing lakes than the two I fished as a kid. Maybe people didn't have the time to fish. There just weren't that many fish caught in the 30s. And they were not as big. I know there were a lot of fish netted for food, but sport fishing was not very active.

Enough old-time fishing history talk. I remember the first big 26-pound northern pike caught in the early 40s at Blue Dog Lake that was showed off in Webster. What a story that was—and remember, I don't write fiction. They all have factual backgrounds.

My brother Ed and his buddies, Lawrence Geis and Eddie Olson, all hard working regular guys—and by regular I don't mean they had prune juice for breakfast, either. Sunday afternoon they headed for Blue Dog Lake to fish. They had the best fishing tackle they could afford, which wasn't much. Secondhand hand-me-down rods and reels, knotted fishing line, lots of energy and a little beer. Arriving at the lake they were a little north of the Blue Dog inlet on the east side, casting Dare Devils. The first thing Eddie Olson caught was a coil of barb wire fence with old 20-pound test line. He was able to pull it in close enough to save his Dare Devil before it snapped back into the lake. Then Lawrence caught a hammer handle size northern. At least they weren't skunked. Then my brother Ed hooked into what he thought was a big fish that almost pulled the rod right out of his hand. Eddie hollered, "Don't horse him in. Let out some line." About that time Ed's rod broke off; all he had was the rod handle and reel, his thumb was bleeding from the line being pulled off the reel so fast.

Lawrence thought Ed had hooked the barb wire Eddie caught earlier until he saw a giant splash and the biggest fish he ever saw broke water.

Then, zing! The center of Ed's old reel went flying out in the water. Ed, now horsing the fish hand-over-hand on the fishing line, rod broken, reel gone and the biggest fish in the lake about to break the line or pull him into the lake. Finally, the big northern pike was in two feet of water, Eddie and Lawrence up to their knees kicking the fish to shore. Its mouth was as big as an alligator—the biggest northern pike these guys had ever seen was headed for Webster. It was show off time. Alfred Hagen of the

Elevator Store opened up to weigh it—26 pounds, some ounces—and all three guys, Ed Bartos, Eddie Olson and Lawrence Geis claimed credit for landing it.

Next day, Ed went into Blackie Fellbaum's hardware store to get a new rod and reel and tell Blackie the story—and he wanted good enough tackle to hold a big fish.

Fact is, Ed never caught another big fish on that outfit. It would be in the mid 1960s on the Missouri near Pierre that was attracting Webster fishermen with lunker northern pike catches. These same three buddies would come back to Webster with five or six 15-21 pound northern pike, hang them on a tree and take pictures of their big catch. But the northern pike they will always remember, was the fish trip 12 miles down the road at Blue Dog Lake when they caught the 26 pounder, not the 500 mile round trip to Pierre which produced sure catches of fish—big by all standards. The show off part of fishing is gone with the years, because everyone catches big fish today. There's more time to fish, better equipment and big fish are common.

Almost all my fishing buddies today have a big fish mounted hanging on the wall—depending on the wife, maybe hanging in the basement or garage. Mine hangs in a bedroom used for storage, somewhat like my mounted elk horns, which I thought would look good in the kitchen, on which my wife could hang dish towels. Those ended up displayed in our outside entry way.

Enough said.

My first deer with a master hunter

Coffee talk at the counter which I serviced when I was a 14-year-old made me aware of most of Main Street accounts and no-accounts—those respected and disrespected. Mostly Main Street businessmen, mayor, councilmen, movers and shakers, men making and developing the town into what it would become, all wore white shirts, ties, suits and hats.

One of these men, unknown to me at the time, would become one of my best and most respected hunting buddies. A man who would always wear a white shirt—even under his hunting clothes. Yet after a lifetime of hunting, I know of no man who understood wildlife in every form—feathered, furred, haired or their habitat as well as he did. And that included human nature as well. He not only researched the history of wildlife, he actually went to Alaska, Africa, Canada, Mexico, all over the US and hunted. Even today few people in this community know of the world records in trophy wildlife he holds. Like the Grand Slam Ram—four species of goats—Rocky Mountain, Alaskan, Desert—a record only a few renown hunters have achieved. A couple of warthog world records in Africa, not counting a 541 pound black bear, a Colorado trophy he let me shoot, that he tracked and guided me to over 50 years ago.

A wildlife man, you would never expect existed as he walked down Main Street. Neatly dressed, respectful to everyone, especially the ladies, as was his gentlemanly custom, his thumb and forefinger would gently touch the brim of his hat as he addressed or met any women on the street. They admired his politeness and courteous manner. And most men respected his judgment and elected him councilman, mayor and president of most clubs in Webster. An asset not only to his business but to the community as well. As a World War I veteran he had also served his nation honorably. Johan Richmond Fiksdal, the man I knew as Mr. Rich

Fiksdal, the funeral director, was soon to reveal another side of his character, a side that was almost hidden from the general public, to me.

Arriving home from WWII some 50 years ago and shortly after a local Legion meeting of which Rich was a prominent member, he asked if I was applying for a deer license at Waubay Waterfowl Refuge—the first lottery deer hunt to reduce the deer population, the first of its kind in Day County. I, like a lot of other guys, had never shot a deer. He went on to explain this was a special hunt. He had an extra application I should fill out and he would submit it with his. The $7 license fee I could pay him later if we were lucky in the drawing. It was to be only a two-day hunt.

My name was third drawn, Rich Fiksdal's was seventh. As we left city hall, where the drawing was held, now the fun begins. Planning the hunt, he said, "Got a shotgun? This hunt requires shotgun slugs. Ever shot slugs?" I didn't even own a shotgun. I really didn't have the license fee yet. No problem. Rich had extra guns I could use. He had extra slugs. He told me how to dress and provided me with his extra hunting clothes and gear. He said to wear a cotton shirt, my army wool shirt, a sweater and his extra red wool hunting coat. He was the best teacher I ever had. Every free moment, I got up to Rich's store to talk about the hunt.

"What's your wife think about this hunting trip?" "We ain't going anyplace except Waubay. What do you mean," I asked. " Well, I know you've only been married a few months and marriages are made in heaven, but so is thunder and lightning. And there's nothing that can ruin a hunting trip more than knowing the guy you're hunting with is going to catch hell when he comes home." I was shocked! I'm no wimp. I'm the man of my marriage, I thought. Then he gently told me if we are going to hunt for two days and your wife is going to take your place at the cafe, you better find a way to replace her work with a little enjoyment—like we'll be having. Do something nice for her before and after the hunt also. Something I have to be thinking about too.

Being extra nice only made my new wife feel I must have done something really bad to be acting so out of my usual relationship. And she flat out asked what I was up to. Telling her the truth, that Rich said I should be nice before and after the hunt, she laughed and said she would settle for a better light above the bathroom mirror. She got it at once. Telling Rich what happened, his reply was, "You over-did it."

The day I shot my first deer, one of over 30 in over 40 years of hunting, will always be my most memorable, just like Rich had predicted over 50 years ago. I would pass up three or four shots, because Rich said he remembered his first deer and I would too. It was about my last chance, sitting with Rich on a deer crossroads trail about a mile south of Waubay Refuge headquarters. He looking west, me east, I heard Rich's low whispered whistle. Turning there in front of me appeared the biggest buck I've ever seen. I know I fired from the hip, as the deer jumped high in the air. A second shot—a back up—and the deer fell dead. Rich said, "Nice shot Bob. You got your first deer." "No, I didn't, I shot from the hip and this is a shoulder shot. Rich, you got it." "We'll see," Rich said. Lifting up the deer's head, right in the center of the chest was my hip shot. "Great shot, Bob," Rich said, "even if a little buck fever was mixed in."

I've hunted with doctors, but none could surpass Rich's skills in dressing out a deer. If I didn't realize it then I would years later, that he was a master hunter.

My first deer was a 151-pound four-pointer, average at most. I would have it mounted and displayed at Christmas with a red light on his nose as Rudolph.

Ridding the county
of excess jack rabbits

Some 52 years ago jack rabbits were overrunning Day County. There wasn't a farmer in the county who wasn't affected. Every tree grove or windbreak planted was girdled and dying by the hungry jack rabbits. Alfalfa stacks were the hardest hit, to say nothing of summer crops. but this is a winter story. Farmers would surround alfalfa stacks with a lath snow fence, leaving an opening. At night they would drive out and close it, trapping over 20 rabbits inside, dispatching them with clubs. (Dennis Reiprich recalls that.) Driving down the road at night the ditches were full of running jack rabbits. You could hardly drive a mile on the road without hitting one.

The American Legion, VFW and church congregations organized rabbit drives. They surrounded a section of land with 50-60 people with shotguns, walking to the center shooting hundreds of rabbits. They were loaded in grain box trucks and sold for 90¢-$1 apiece. The fur was used in making dress hats and gloves, carcasses sold to mink and fox farms. It was a great money maker for farm kids and fund raiser.

To a lot of us WWII veterans, walking sections of land and haystack climbing was sort of a lot of work, so about 15 of us guys decided to make a hunting sport out of rabbit hunting. harold Hagen, Jack Vincent, Jeff Nelson, me and my brothers, Fred Haase and sometimes his sons, Neil and Arlo, and others, walked small tree strips. One was out north of Bill Kanago's farm. Walking beside Fred Haase among the shotgun blasts, he suddenly fell to his knees. He was hit by shotgun pellets, breaking the nosepiece on his glasses, a few pellets buried in his forehead, bleeding. His sons, remember that happening. Neil is a retired air force and airline pilot, Arlo a longtime game warden in the Milbank area.

That sort of ended tree hunting, so we started hunting over a spread out wide area of fields using .22 rifles. This was how airplane rabbit hunting was invented. Oh! What a sport that was—and it will never exist again. Here's how it developed and happened.

Jeff Nelson was part of our hunting group and we thought he got lost—after an hour of waiting he showed up. It was cold and the ground was covered with snow. Asking how many rabbits he shot, he said, "I must have 30 piled up back there. I ran out of shells." Almost breathless he continued, "I was in this willow patch and Jack Faulkenberg (the pilot instructor in webster) flew over us. Every rabbit in this quarter of land came running into the willow patch for cover. Where I was! I got about three or four coming in. They were nuts—they would jump right over me. After the plane left, out they ran and I'd get a few more. I couldn't load the rifle fast enough. When the plane came back again, here they came again. They must have thought that plane was a big eagle or owl or something."

Planning the next hunt, about 20 of us would spread out in a grove of trees located in a section of land northwest of what's now Leonard Naessig's farm. Using our airplane Jeff would circle the land around the grove to see if the same results would happen.

Next day, everyone, with .22 automatic rifles loaded with hollow point bullets and three or four boxes of shells, lined up in the trees. Flying 50 feet off the ground, here comes the plane. Rabbits were jumping up from the fields by the hundreds, running for the cover of the trees, straight at us. Guys shooting their automatics, rabbits falling. It sounded like 10 German machine guns rat-a-tatting, pop! pop! On came the rabbits into the tree grove, jumping over the kneeling hunters, out the other side of the grove they ran. We hardly had time to reload our guns when the plane circled the other side and back came the rabbits, heading into the tree grove again. This went on for about an hour and the shoot was over. Then came the work. Picking up hundreds of rabbits, loading them into vehicles of the day—old WWII surplus Jeeps, international four-wheel scouts and some pickups. We had developed a new way to rid the county of the overpopulation of destructive jack rabbits. Or at least somewhat control them.

Soon, Myron Roth invented a car hood sled (an old car hood turned upside down) which made picking up shot rabbits a lot easier. almost all of us got one. Sunday we would fill a grain box truck full of a couple hundred rabbits, selling them to Bauske's and Wist Produce or other fur buyers. Half the proceeds went for airplane gas, the rest for .22 shells. And a little for the hunting party afterwards.

This type of rabbit hunting lasted for only a couple of years, then the fox overpopulation took over.

Times change. You still see quite a few fox, but seldom a jack rabbit. And there will always be that group of dummies who blame the hunter. Like the hunters killed all the buffalo. Well, can you imagine today a small herd of buffalo in Day County—running over the soybean and corn fields. No way! We have too many geese, cormorants, pelicans, raptures. Hunting is the only orderly way to reduce any one species of wildlife. As for yesterday's old saying, "Mother nature will take care of it," forget it! Man has long ago built and farm cultivated Mother Nature out of it. Pasture land and the poorest ground is productive with herbicides and fertilizers. Times have changed. If geese interfere with airplanes, geese must go, not airplanes. If coons and skunks interfere too much with our pheasant population they will go also. yesterday, man adapted to Mother Nature. Today, Mother Nature adapts to man, as does her wildlife. Think about it! Deer overrun Rapid City, geese overrun Pierre and the airports. Coons raid garbage cans. Solutions to those problems will be man-made to serve man—not wildlife. It just hasn't all happened yet!

Out of a job—
goose season closed

The goose season in Eastern South Dakota is closed, but it's still open along the river at Pierre. For me and my 75-80 year old hunting buddies its like losing our jobs. We hunt almost every day in goose hunting season. It's our full time job in retirement. It's our exercise. It keeps us young. At least that's the excuse to our wives as we are buying shells and hunting stuff, wrecking the family budget. Somebody's got to do it. Just think of all the young unemployed game and fish guys if we didn't hunt.

The worst days to hunt are weekends because all the young guys are off work. It's less competition because we miss a lot of shots. I think the old guys just like to shoot. We are slow to react, can't see like we used to. None of us can hear the geese coming or honking. They all count on the law of averages. If you shoot up enough steel shot something is bound to come down. Every flock of geese gets three shots aimed or not.

We just couldn't resist the idea goose season had ended, yet 200 miles away it was still open. We just didn't want the season to end for us. With a call to old friends in Pierre, telling us the goose hunting was great there lots of geese, we somehow talked the wives out of half the monthly food budget and at 5 a.m., off we went.

After about four hours of driving heading down Highway 1804 about eight miles north of Pierre we saw flocks of geese crossing the road and a public shooting area parking lot with five or six pickups. We drove in.

There were two hunters with a limit of geese. AFter talking to them we couldn't get our shells and guns out fast enough. As we headed for their vacant spots on the bluffs, after a three block run (in our case a fast walk) us old guys were breathless we got to our spot. Other hunters along the bluff line yelled o get down as a flock of over 100 geese headed for us off the river below us.

As they went over us we saluted the high flyers with a three shot volley. And to our surprise, one dropped out about 50 yards in back of it. No time to retrieve it, the other hunters were hollering, Here they come! Get down! Another flock! This time my buddy and I gave them our three shot salute and two more dropped out. That was one limit for us and we were there only 10 minutes. But before we could go out and pick up our geese a couple of young hunters who had dropped a couple of geese also picked up ours, joking, telling us after we thanked them that it's better for all the hunters if us slow old guys just stayed put rather than taking half an hour to retrieve our geese and scaring the flocks so nobody gets a shot.

About this time another old guy was leaving and he didn't have a goose. He just missed the only good shot he had all morning, but was hoping he could get one for his neighbor who had guests staying with him. We asked if he would like a couple of ours. We made him very happy. We still had another day to hunt and we would give our geese to neighbors and friends who would enjoy them anyway.

That would also make our wives happy. My wife says, Why don't you shoot a roast beef? I'd enjoy that. Sometimes I don't understand why you hunt. You don't eat one a season, you just give them away. And most of the time you don't even get a shot. Getting up at 5 in the morning, going out in the freezing cold. If someone was paying you to do it you would quit right away.

After 56 years of marriage you would think she would understand and she really does. Comments like that come natural from an old goose hunter's wife. She knows that hunting is an in-bred thing. A habit good or bad that stays with a man to his dying day. Maybe that's why they call us old guys die hard goose hunters.

I should have never commented on my wife's goose hunting remarks, because I'm going to end up losing and in some trouble. Because there is no good reason or answer that an old hunter can come up with and the wife makes a lot of good points in her comments.

First of all, my wife hunted with me before marriage and about a year after. She was the only gal in our group. We expected her to bring lunch, but we soon found out she could shoot pretty good also even if she was placed in poor spots of the duck flight. There wasn't much goose hunting back then. I know she felt out of place in an all man group, but that all ended when the babies started arriving. It's pretty hard to get a babysitter at five in the morning. For over 50 years she was too busy with household stuff doing double duty when I hunted. Now that the kids are grown and gone, I suggested she start hunting again. And that's how it all started. I'm about to tell you part of it.

How many 75 year old women have you seen out hunting? I had to admit I had never seen one, but it's hard to tell a woman's age in a down filled parka. Everyone looks alike. Well now, she says. The only place I seen women dressed in hunting clothes is in cafes with young guys about your grandson's age. I'm not going to win this conversation! So I quit.

My wife still makes a great hunting lunch gets up and makes breakfast for me, wishes me good shooting and be careful as I leave for my daily goose hunt. But if I think I'm going to get her to turn back the clock of time, when it was all duck and no goose hunting, when she played dog, retrieving birds and only getting to shoot at the tail end of the flock, expecting her to prepare the perfect lunch, help clean and cook the game. Forget it. Those days by her standards are long gone. She still drives the pickup pheasant hunting and easy things like that. But for freezing her butt waiting for a goose shot again, forget it.

Those days are gone and I better understand her point of view. I know her coffee click gals will laugh heir whole gab session when she tells them about the dumb hunting idea her husband came up with asking her to go goose hunting again.

Somehow, I thought it was a good idea. At least she knows I like having her around even in goose hunting season. I'll get all her support for my goose hunting habit but only while she can remain in a warm place inside. Not in the freezing cold windy ditch or goose pit waiting for a goose shot. Now that's my job. By myself and hunting buddies with her warm inside support.

What more can an 80 year old hunter ask for in life?

Webster's hobo jungle and the KKK

The history of Webster will record that we were a great medical center, electrical supplier for the area and many other great things citizens of our county can be proud of. There are also things in our background we would like to hide and forget.

Like one that affected all of Day County and our state, when South Dakota was made propaganda capitol of the nation in promoting steel shot for waterfowl hunting. As an old time pass shooting hunter I'm not proud of that crippling fact at all.

Not everyone will agree with that statement on steel shot, but here's one everyone would like to see excluded from Webster's history. The following story is mostly taken from the 1925 Reporter & Farmer, plus my personal talks with former KKK members. They were mostly Webster businessmen, prominent area farmers and WWI vets.

In 1925 Webster was a growing community of hard working homesteaders and businessmen who were well established and doing well. WWI was over and Webster was growing faster than it could cope with. Elements of people were passing through town, immigrants wanted to enjoy our new country but were reluctant to give up their old country ways, wanting original inhabitants of the area to match their ways.

Regardless of what country you came from, you're American now. You'll speak English, send your kids to school, attend church and your word better be as good as your credit. Each family will be a giver, not a taker in the area you live, or we don't want you here. This was the attitude that prevailed in Webster. New arrivals were told outright, "This is America, blend in. Don't stand out using old country speech and customs. Your new life and home is America!"

There were some followers of a loud mouthed guy, trying to change original laws, traveling in a wagon train in northeast Day County. The sheriff was trying to arrest him for treason, according to the 1925 R&F.

Wagon loads of gypsies with dancing girls, soil doves of the day and night, pickpockets were making weekly trips through the county. Webster had a hobo jungle, that was the half way stop made of tin and cardboard shacks where Watertown Co-op Elevator is now, with 15-20 hobos and tramps coming and going daily. Gangs of six or seven would raid local gardens of vegetables, push people around begging for money and in bars bumming drinks and fighting. It was getting out of hand for law enforcement. We didn't have jail holding capacity.

Even good German Americans within the Webster area were being harassed because they received a letter or sent a package to family members back home. Things were out of hand.

Webster was ripe for some silver tongued organizer from out of town to take advantage of its despair—under the guise of Americanism, the Ku Klux Klan was formed.

Now I quote from the Reporter & Farmer, April 23, 1925—"A speaker for the Ku Klux Klan held forth at the opera house Monday evening to a good sized crowd. We fail to find many who were greatly impressed with the necessity for such an organization."

Again from the R&F, "Tuesday night at about 11 o'clock a fiery cross was burned on the lower end of Main Street. It was a large cross and illuminated that section of the city for quite a time. Whether it was the work of the Klan or some persons who wished to create a false impression is not known. A second cross was burned Wednesday night, on the north end of Main Street."

July 16, 1925, "Thousands see KKK meeting. Many states represented in gathering to witness session of Klan.

"The largest crowd which ever gathered in Webster attended the demonstration of the Ku Klux Klan on the hill east of the city Monday evening. There was no way to check the number of cars or people who attended but it is generally conceded that in the neighborhood of 2,000 automobiles were present, which would mean at least 5,000 people. In the string of cars were noticed number plates representing many different states and most counties of South Dakota sent representatives.

"The speaker of the evening held a large crowd in front of the platform for more than an hour and received good attention in spite of the fact that cars were moving almost continually nearby which would sometimes make it impossible to follow the address. His topic was Americanism and was covered thoroughly, containing many things every good citizen should bear in mind.

"Perhaps the greatest attraction for visitors was the display of fireworks and burning of crosses. The display of fireworks, while not particularly large, was very beautiful and burning of three Ks and three crosses presented a spectacular sight against the dark sky about midnight.

"Curiosity was perhaps the great magnet which swelled the crowd to the largest ever gathered here at this first demonstration given in this section."

Sept. 10, 1925, R&F, again I quote, "The Methodist Episcopal Church Sunday evening was attended by about 25 members of the Ku Klux Klan in full regalia. One of the members in a few well chosen remarks presented to the church a beautiful silk US flag as a mark of respect to B.D. Fish, only surviving veteran of the Civil War in our city, a member of this church. He also presented to the church a substantial sum of money for its kindly attitude toward the Klan. The address by Rev. Bullock, '100 percent American, who are they?' was an able effort and much appreciated by the large audience. Appropriate music added much to the very fine program.

Now, my comments. That hill located a mile east on Highway 12 still bears scars of the cross dug into it 76 years ago. I'm reminded of some past history every time I drive by it—but I believe no one was ever hurt. It was more or less part of a big propaganda promotion under the guise of good old fashioned Americanism. I can name some of the officers of that 40-member group—and most of them were Main Street businessmen, prominent farmers and church people.

With no worthwhile goal except to keep tramps and hobos on passing freight trains from overstaying their welcome, with the help of the Klan, law enforcement soon came well under control. The club with white hoods soon came to an end—after they heard of the ruthlessness of southern Klans and the way they operated—and was never heard from again in this area. But I'm sure even in the late 70s most Webster people did business with former Klan members. Old businessmen never made public their membership in the KKK. And much like some of our past history, we would rather forget and erase because of the KKK reputation gained from areas other than Webster.

Being part of the KKK—a fact no one wants to talk about or believe really existed. Yet it's part of our history that can't be erased. It operated and existed.

52

Things aren't like they used to be

Raining—windy—cold October morning. As the old guys limp into the cafe for morning coffee and daily old-time talk, giving their verbal voicing of old-time solutions to modern day problems. Sometimes it's funny, sometimes it's just meaningless old-time memories that no one has thought of in over 60 years. That's longer than most other people in the cafe were born.

Their talk is only important to the old guys at the table. Most of the people in the cafe couldn't care less about the past. It's more important to them what today and tomorrow bring. The old guys think in terms of trust your future to a proven past. Now, for this day's coffee talk.

About eight old guys sipping coffee, a few more coming to join the group. Nothing was being said when one speaks. Lucky Strike green has gone to war—remember that? And the Lucky Strike hit parade? Know what? Lucky Strike green never returned after the war. There must be 100 different brands of cigarettes in the stores. Most I've never heard of. Oh, they still have Lucky Strikes in the white pack with the red label, but where are the old brands I knew? Like Wings, Chesterfields, Spuds, Herbert Tarringtons and the flat 50 packs. Never see them anymore.

That statement got the old memory wheels turning in the rest of the old guys' heads. Yeah, said another guy. You never see plug tobacco either, anymore. Brands like Right Cut, Pay Day, Spark Plug, Day's Work, Horseshoes. I wonder if they still make it. They were big sellers, too. Well, they still got Copenhagen snuff. I see that on display. Sure I want it, but I don't need it. In my day it cost 10 cents a box or 80 cents a roll of 10 boxes. Now it's $3.50 a box with tax. A roll costs $33.00—that's 35 times what it was 60 years ago and they haven't made it any better than it was back then, either.

Another old guy said the same thing is true about booze. About the only old-time booze in the liquor store we couldn't afford was Four Roses and Jack Daniels. Brands we bought in half pints and pints were Three Feathers, P.M. (nicknamed post mortem and puke and moan) and Harvest Time. They were cheap to 50 cents. Now they no longer exist. Now days all you see is fancy name brands that sell from 10 to 20 times what a guy could buy a pint for 60 years ago. Half pints they don't even sell anymore. They just push the quart size stuff.

Now the old-time memory wheels were really turning. Everyone had something to say. Mostly what a $5 weekly check would buy compared to today's prices—where minimum wage is more than that for one hour's work with a 10 minute break.

Yeah! Getting back to the Lucky Strike hit parade. That was music. You had to be a professional musician back then. They had to read music, play by note and band arrangements. Nowadays all you have is a bunch of painted up clowns banging on drums and amplified string guitars, making a boom, boom noise. They call that music! And kids pay $65 a ticket just to yell and holler at them and get their eardrums busted. I just don't understand it.

Well now! Another old guy speaks up. I remember back in 1938 when the big band sounds first started. And jitterbug dancing. My folks said the same thing you're talking about. They grew up with waltz and polka music. All guitar ballad stuff. They thought we were nuts too. It didn't make any sense to my folks either. Songs like String of Pearls, Elmer's Tune, In the Mood, Take the A Train. Just like the Beatles' boom boom music don't make sense to us old guys. Maybe it is just a good sign of old age. My folks used to talk about what my grandparents said about the jazz era that they lived through also. What goes around comes around, I guess.

Look, another old guy interrupts. Look at the price of gas. I remember when it was 18 cents a gallon. Now it's $1.50 and there's talk about $2 a gallon. Another old guy gets into the talk. There's 43 cents tax on it. That's three times what you paid for it. You'll never see 18 cent gas again. Go to the grocery store. People are paying 79 cents for a 32 oz. bottle of plain drinking water. And a new car costs five times what I paid for my house.

Just then a young guy joins our table—a guy about 63 or 64, about ready to retire. His comments were about to change a lot of old guys thinking from past to present. Or would it?

The young guy speaks. You guys talking about old times doesn't make a lot of sense. Look, 60 years ago most of you were making an average salary of 50-60 dollars a month. Some of you were buying land for 10-20 dollars an acre. Today you're all drawing social security checks for 12-15 times more a month than you made back then. The land you bought sells for at least 20 times what you paid for it. In fact, even the house you improved and updated sells for 10 times what you paid for it after living in it for 25-30 years. and for the price of gas and its 43 cent tax, look at the paved roads and bridges it's brought. Compare that to the old dirt trails and gravel roads. Loose gravel caused most of the wrecks, even traveling at 30 miles per hour caused serious accidents. Remember when you saw a car raising a little dust, someone would say, "There he goes trying to beat 60." Today you drive 60 on the highway and everybody is passing you. At that, the young guy pays for his coffee and leaves.

None of the old guys said much. Until one said, "That young guy never said a damn thing we don't already know." I wonder who told him about cars going to beat 60. A common phrase 60 years ago, he couldn't have been but three or four years old then. I enjoyed our-old time talk this morning, and I'm sure in another 15 years that young guy will be talking about the 60s and 70s like we are about the 30s and 40s, and the many changes that most of us won't live to see. Proves one thing—what goes around comes around with each generation.

And with that, the old guys' morning session ends. No funny stuff, just a lot of meaningless old-time talk. But every one of the old guys was happy about one thing. Their brains were still active. Even if the rest of their bodies were aging. They were happy, looking forward to tomorrow. Happy to be Americans, knowing they have served and helped develop the America we live in today. Knowing its foundation may be shaken, but will never crumble to any change or problem it may face.

53

Coffee session takes mind off problems

As I walked into the cafe for coffee with the old guys, I felt pretty rejected. I'd been skunked in three days of goose hunting, I was sick of hearing about anthrax on TV. The old guys had been talking and thinking serious as true Americans for weeks now—about the war on terrorism and setbacks to our American way of life. It was time to relax, be alert and support the younger guys who are taking care of this problem that's hurting our freedom. Something like us old guys did taking care of past problems.

It was about time the old guys stopped fearing fear itself and started doing something to improve morale. That's something we are still capable of doing—our fighting days are long past—and by the sounds of laughter coming from the old guys' table they were priming themselves for the task ahead. To change the serious mood to a lighter one. We old guys already knew something about enemies of freedom and the mosquito bites of terrorism that have stung our American way of life. But our slap back is going to make the world a better place to live—after the mosquito biting terrorists are dead.

Old time talk, jokes and laughter were in full swing when I joined the old guys' coffee table. "What's all the laughter about?" I asked. Well, old Fred drank too much coffee, went to the bathroom and came back with his barn door open. Another guy told him, "You forgot to zip up." Old Fred retorted, "It could have been worse. I could have forgot to zip it down!"

That started it. Someone feeling sorry for old Fred said, Hey Wally! I noticed you had a little trouble parking your car. That's a sign of old age. Yeah! Wally said I had that problem when I was younger too, just getting a girl to agree to it. The old guys were on a roll this morning.

Someone made a remark about things getting tougher when you get over the hill. Around the table came all kinds of comments like, it's better to be over the hill enjoying the view than under it. A lot of guys never made it to the top.

By now I was really enjoying this coffee time, but then the whole coffee group turned on me. You know what they say about old golfers. They chase that white ball because they are too old to chase anything else. And a few more comments I think better left unwritten.

My only retort was to change the subject and get on somebody else. Hey Joe! Golf isn't as bad as your goose hunting. Your hunting buddy said he saw a flock of geese headed low right over your goose blind. You took a shot, then another shot and by the time you put the bottle down they were gone!

Just then old "Doc" joined the group and they were really primed for him. He doesn't believe in acupuncture. He likes to stick us with the bill. Old Doc was pretty awake with his comeback, too. Mother Nature makes mistakes too—giving big mouths to people who have the least to say.

The whole coffee group was interrupted by the sassy waitress refilling coffee cups when one old guy asked for a glass of water. The waitress brought it and said, "Well, what do you say?" Lifting the glass the old guy looked her straight in the eye and said, "Cheers!" And the old guys' laughing talk started all over again.

A young guy, hearing all the laughter at the old guys' table, tried to quiet the group with some comments of his own. You know, you old guys are America's biggest carrier of aids—hearing aids, band aids, medical aids, government aids… Look, Sonny, one old guy responds, we don't mind being 75 or 80 years old. A lot of people are denied the privilege. And remember this, at our age there are seven or eight women for every old guy. And we don't miss many opportunities because our hearing aids are never turned off. We got a lot of living to do, and the laughter roars again.

I really should be leaving for home, but I hate to leave first because then you become the butt of the hen peck wife jokes—and the guys are really sharp today.

Sure enough, another old guy grabs his check and reaches in his pocket for tip change. Of course everyone notices, and the remarks start flowing about the early leaver. Statements like, "I don't know why Joe is going home so quick. His wife has been wrapping his hunting lunch in road maps all week." Another guy, "My wife always gets the last word."

"You're lucky, mine never does." Now, the wife jokes start. My wife and I went out to eat the other night. I suggested she try the special shrimp plate. "No," she said, "Shrimp doesn't agree with me." My comment was, "My dear, it wouldn't dare." And I'm sure a lot of you guys lied on your income tax return when you listed yourselves as head of household.

Well, enough of this old time talk and jokes. I'm going to have to leave the coffee table. And as I do, so are most of the other guys. This is one morning coffee session I forgot all about my rejected feelings and am smiling at all the old-time jokes I'd forgotten. One thing for sure, the old guys are very alert and their minds are quick at coffee time. I would like to call the old guys old gentlemen, but somehow after hearing some of the old jokes this morning, it's better for me to just say old guys. Because some of the jokes are unprintable.

Every town has to be known by something

Seventy some years ago Webster was known as "The City of Trees." The Better Webster Club used that slogan on postcards.

Driving anywhere from entering Main Street from the north to all side streets, it was like driving through a tunnel of leaves and branches. Somewhat like driving down Ninth Avenue West today.

But with new homes, businesses and recreation area construction, tree age and diseases this is no longer true. What made the slogan so meaningful was after the dirty 30s a real effort was made to plant trees on every farm to protect and hamper soil erosion and dust storms. The city of Webster's trees already existed and were a marvel to see.

Years later Webster was known as "The Petunia Capital of the World." Planted petunias and signs entering town proclaimed that fact. Webster Junior Chamber of Commerce sponsored that slogan.

But the one slogan that's best remembered was sponsored by Mother Nature and the Webster Sewer Department. It probably gave Webster more claim to fame and was better known throughout all the area for many years. Even up to the present time by old-timers. There was a sign east of Webster on old Highway 12 known as the Yellowstone Trail, now 12th Avenue going past the swimming pool and across the golf course. The sign said, "Welcome to Webster." It was located just east of the sewer ditch bridge. Well now! About a quarter of a mile before you reached the sewer ditch you could start to smell it, even with the window up on the car. By the time you reached the welcome to Webster sign the stink was unbearable. Even on breezy days it didn't matter. The smell lingered like a cloud of foul smelling stuff coming from a freshly used outhouse somewhat mixed with the smell of an overcrowded, unventilated hog or sheep shed in lambing season. The sewer ditch smell could put the worst smell you can think of to shame.

By the time you reached the bridge that crossed the sewer ditch and the Welcome to Webster sign most people had watering eyes. Even after you passed the bridge the smell followed you into town—on some days the whole town of Webster. When the wind was easterly the stinking smell would be the main topic of conversation. We sort of got used to it, but for newcomers it was a first impression never to be forgotten, but to be put up with.

The city fathers, after years of dredging and cleaning the ditch only made the smell worse. But they somewhat corrected it by placing a new remodeled lagoon, after the old Yellowstone Trail was rerouted north of town to its present location. But the sewer ditch still remains, and even now with spring thaws we get a faint smell that brings back memories of days past. When the wind is in the east, that's when the old guys say it's nothing like it used to be years ago. And it's no wonder to me the Jaycees wanted to improve the welcome to Webster by promoting petunias. I could write a column of those old jokes, but they wouldn't be printable.

In advertising the more of people's five senses you appeal to—sight, sound, touch, taste and smell—the more appealing the response. But the sense of smell was incorporated in the Welcome to Webster sign and it outdid every known advertising campaign ever developed or remembered anywhere on the Yellowstone Trail from Minneapolis to the West Coast.

Even though any town would be embarrassed to have such a stinking welcoming as a sewer ditch entering its town from the east and leaving it from the west, Webster at its stinking best somehow prospered from its smelling entry. We had five or six grocery stores, now we have two. We had three hardware stores, now we have one. We had three great clothing and department stores, now we have none.

Our business thrived on many small farm operations and farmers. Now small diversified farms hardly exist. In those days every farm had a hog shed and a few milk cows. So that smell to them on the farm meant money. As for city slickers traveling through town, it was a disgusting, stinking smell to put up with. Most of those people spent little money in Webster businesses, but they all talked about the Welcome to Webster sign and the smell at the entry of Webster, which made Webster, SD a well known place.

Somehow South Dakotans have a way of tuning bad points people see in our state into great assets. Just mentioning Webster's smelling sewer ditch brought us free advertising—somewhat like Wall did with its miles of worthless wasteland now called the South Dakota Badlands—a nationwide tourist attraction.

I've got a lot of well-known out of state friends who don't understand small town living , but they love to hunt pheasants, ducks and geese here. Our lakes and fishing bring hundreds of out of staters here and they enjoy it. But there's something about going into a small town cafe for a local guy and knowing everybody there, talking and listening so much your coffee gets cold. I'll just say I love it here and end this column saying bad things are remembered longer than good things. But even dark clouds turn sunny most times in our towns and lives.

Lazy Bones and his cottage on the lake

Back in the 1930s and 40s, even though I was just a guest or visitor I knew almost every cottage owner, its location on Pickerel Lake and the girls who lived there. They were local area people and maybe a few from Aberdeen. All the cottages had names. Most of those cottages and their owners no longer exist or the cottages have been improved beyond recognition. Hundreds of new ones have been built by people living hundreds of miles from our local area.

A few that still exist, that I can recall offhand, were Trail's End (the Fiksdal family cottage) and the present day 4-EEE (that of the Vander Linden family). Gone are the names Kozy Cabin, 4-Comfort, Apple Sauce, Dew Drop In, Breeze In, On-Pa-Wee Lodge, This Wil Do, Lettuce Loaf In, No-Mor-Woes and No Ambish.

A couple of new cottage signs I've seen a painting of a worm on a hook called De-bate. A lawyer from Minneapolis owns that one. Also, there is a painted sign of a duck, Duck In. Otherwise cottage names are a thing mostly of the past. But the most remembered cottage name and sign was a small wooden sign on Mink Bedessem's cottage, Lazy Bones, on the south end of Pickerel. And that's what this story is mostly about. How Mink Bedessem's cottage got its name.

It all started in the depression era when Webster was doing what would nowadays be called politically incorrect. Professional and Main Street businessmen would sponsor a three-night minstrel show in Liberty Theater. It was all local talent, all original, all amateur. It was and would be the most laughable fund raiser that ever existed a yearly event that will be remembered 50-60 years afterwards.

After weeks of rehearsal, opening night found the Liberty Theater packed to standing room only crowds. And there on stage, about 30 doctors and businessmen, faces painted black, top hats, white gloves, white shirts and bow ties singing the popular songs of the day accompanied by the best local pit orchestra. After the singing was a comedy skit which would never grow old. Everyone knew it by heart. It would bring a roar of laughter that stopped the show for five or 10 minutes. For years the skit was performed by Dr. Pfister, Dr. Karlins, Dr. Caldwell and Art Lindquist.

The scene, break time in the doctors' lounge; setting, Peabody Hospital. And they couldn't find a deck of cards to play poker. So they had to improvise by using what was on hand. It seems the hospital staff would place sign cards on most of the patient room doors to prepare the nurses for what they were entering and what was going on inside. Like scarlet fever, diphtheria, small pox or whatever. And using this makeshift deck of cards, the poker game begins. And the ending is, Well, what have you got? I've got two appendicitis. No good! I've got three small pox. The last guy says, I won, I won! I've got four enemas! The rest of the players in the skit all yell, Take the pot. You'll need it! and the roar of laughter.

On with the show. Another song, Stop, Look and Listen. Black face Eddie Nerger with a big stop sign, flashing it every time Stop came up in the vocal. And a guy dressed as a gal in a swimsuit appears on stage every time Look comes up in the song. And all the singing group has earhorns to use when Listen comes up. My writing can't do it justice.

Well, getting back to the cottage named Lazy Bones. Doc Anderson reminded me of this. There was a group of eight, shall I say overweight, business guys who were great singers. Instead of being known as an octet they called themselves the ox tet and they would sing the popular songs of the day. Lazy Bones, sleepin' in the sun, how you expect to get your day's work done. And Mink Bedessem, lounging in shorts, legs crossed in the air waving in time with the lyrics of the song with a drink in one hand and a smoke in the other, straw hat cocked. He so enjoyed making people laugh. And his role in the show, long after it was over, had people coming in the barber shop calling him lazy bones. So he named his cabin at Pickerel Lake after the character he loved playing so much. And the little wooden sign remained as long as the cabin stood for over 30 years.

The minstrel show was a yearly event. Original every year, but the skit of the doctors' poker game and the song Lazy Bones (long after it was no longer a hit) remained a standard part of every show.

In hard times like the dirty 30s it took a lot to get people to forget and laugh a much needed therapy in that era. I miss the black face minstrel shows, Norwegian, Swedish, Jewish and Polish jokes by people of that nationality. I always felt left out because there were no Bohemian jokes. So much for thin skin politically incorrect stuff in Day County South Dakota.

After rereading this column I found out one thing. I'll never be a theater review writer.